PAINT WORKS

ALTHEA WILSON

with Sally Slaney

Photography by Mark Jones

FAWCETT COLUMBINE
New York

To My Family

Design/Paul Bowden and Elizabeth Ayer
Illustrations/Rodney Paull
Althea Wilson's make-up/Jane Goddard

A Fawcett Columbine Book
Published by Ballantine Books

Library of Congress Cataloging-in-Publication Data

Wilson, Althea, *1948–*
   Paint works.

      1. House painting – Amateurs' manuals.   2. Interior
   decoration – Amateurs' manuals.   I. Title.
   TT323.W54   1989   745.7   88-47814
   ISBN 0-449-90291-9

Manufactured in The Netherlands
First American Edition: June 1989
10 9 8 7 6 5 4 3 2 1

(Facing title page) 'Pink lilies in blue and white jug', 1987
(Title page) Peony in a Turkish vase painted on tiles
(Pages 6–7) Chinese plate dado design
(Page 142) 'Watermelon on a Wooden Shelf', 1987

Contents

INTRODUCTION 9

African Roots 9
Individual Influences 12
Sense of Adventure 13

PART ONE: WHERE IT ALL BEGAN 15

CHAPTER ONE: PAINT FINISHES 17

Helpful History 18

Walls 18
Wood Panelling 18
Dados 18
Tiles 21
Furniture 25
Textiles 25

The Contemporary Vision 28

The Importance of Research 28
Achieving the Style 30
Thornton's Panelled Dining Room 30
Georgian Panelled Bedroom 31
Variations on a Theme of Tulips 32
German Secretaire 34
Japanese Bamboo 36
How Lazy Do You Feel? 37
Tree of Life 38
Chinese Plate 39
Two Chinese Style Dining Rooms 40

CHAPTER TWO: DISCUSSION ON PAINT 43

Why I Use Water-based Paints 44
Mixing Paint 44
Brushes for Water-based Paint Finishes 46
Working with Water-based Paints 47
Colour 47
Simple Colour Mixes 49
Texture 49
Pattern 52

PART TWO: MY PAINT TECHNIQUES   55

CHAPTER THREE: WALLS   57

Preparing the Surfaces   58
How to Measure Up Wall Areas for Panelling   58
Treatment of Radiators, Doors and Skirtings   58
Antiquing Effects   61
Sponging   61
Dry Sponging   62
Marbling   62
Grey and White Marbling   63
Black Marbling   64
Battered French   64
Stone Finishes   68
Wood Painted to Look Like Wood   71
Fantasy Wood Graining   72
Stencils and the Way I Use Them   73
Painting on to Glazed Wall Tiles   76

CHAPTER FOUR: FURNITURE   81

Restoration of Painted Furniture   82

Preparation of Surfaces   82
Gilding   82
Metal Finishes   82
Malachite   85
Cutouts or Companions   92
Frames   95

CHAPTER FIVE: TEXTILES   97

New and Old   98
Buying Second-hand   98
Preparing and Dyeing Cloth Prior to Painting   98
Painting Cloth to Look Old   100
Adirẹ Cloth   100
Hand-painted Curtains or Blinds   102
Roller Blinds   102
Gimps   105
Tassels   105
Braid   105
Identification of Historical Textiles   105

CHAPTER SIX: DESIGN RESOURCES   109

Finding Inspiration   110
The Jungle   110
Chinese Water Lily   112
The Tree of Life   115
Bamboo Wall   116

CHAPTER SEVEN: CREATING A ROOM SET   119

The Focal Point   120
A Word About Floors   120
Final Touches   120
How a Disaster Area with Seven Doorways was Transformed   123
Chinese Room Set   124
African Room Set   128
The Drawing Room   128

EPILOGUE   131

STENCILS   133

INDEX   142

LIST OF SUPPLIERS   144

Introduction

There tends to be an enormous amount of mystique surrounding the art of the painted finish. Beginners may look longingly at a piece of marbling or malachite and wish to try it, but be daunted by the sheer complexity of the instructions. I have never been very conscientious about following complicated techniques and in my book I have tried to express my ideas as simply as possible. I am convinced that anyone can produce sophisticated and effective paint finishes, using the methods that are described in these 'recipes'.

The thing is just to paint, remembering that anything you do can always be re-done if you don't like the effect. All you lose is time – and maybe not even that, as you certainly gain in experience, so improving your painting ability. The reason paint plays such a very important part in achieving the overall desired effect in my schemes is because it is one of the cheapest ways of covering walls and other surfaces. Hours of pleasure can be derived from looking around in antique and second-hand shops which then allows ingenuity and imagination free rein.

All the techniques in this book have been achieved using water-based paints: emulsion, gouache or powder. They have a chalky, dull appearance which gives the same effect as old-fashioned lime-based paints, whereas oil-based paints are usually hard and shiny to the eye. I have been lucky, in that I have been encouraged to paint since childhood and have been surrounded by environments which influenced my work.

African Roots

Although I was born and went to school in England, Nigeria was my home for about 25 years and I spent a great part of my childhood in Kano. Crayons, paints and drawing started at an early age, because, to be frank, apart from riding there was little else for children to do.

Kano is the first large city south of the Sahara Desert; consequently the Islamic culture has greatly influenced the architecture, customs, and general attitude towards daily life. The markets, for example, are quiet, cool places run by men, whereas in the south they are almost totally inhabited by women traders, and one really notices the different atmosphere of organized noise and chaos. I remember visiting the ancient indigo pits where you could buy cloth or have your own cloth redyed with a great variety of local designs, still using the old methods.

A kind of chintz is produced in Kano not unlike that imported from 1614 onwards to Europe from India. After the cloth, which is usually cotton, has been dyed in the indigo pits, it is dried and then taken to nearby mud huts. Inside, the huts were usually quite dark and terribly hot, and two men, cross-legged, would sit opposite each other on the well-beaten mud floor with a large tree trunk between them. The cloth was laid out on the tree trunk and the men, with wooden implements similar to a sculptor's mallet, would bash the cloth in unison, with the effect of beating it totally flat and compacting the fibres to form a shining surface. These lengths of cloth, some ten foot by three, would be worn by the proud chieftains and courtiers of the Emir's palace; wound into tightly bound turbans, they shimmered almost silver in the sunlight. This process had to be repeated each time the cloth was washed, taking hours, so I am sure that nobody cleaned it very often!

This is one of my favourite portraits which I called 'The Grey Lady', 1983. The picture was influenced by my obsession with the Elizabethan period, coupled with requests from clients who wanted me to paint 'instant ancestors' for them.

(Far left) A Chieftain's door. Taken from a wooden carving of the Hausa region of northern Nigeria. (Left) Again, this design was influenced by the calabashes or gourds used in everyday Nigerian life for carrying milk and other foodstuffs. These highly decorated vessels are found in the Fulani tribal area of the north.

Kano is a city of red dust, and has the largest remaining mud-brick city wall in Africa, which the British would not allow to be repaired during their occupation for fear that the city would regain its famed impregnability. The old part of the city including the Emir's palace was built of the local red earth, made into bricks by hand and baked in the sun. The Emir's palace always reminded me of what medieval Europe must have been like with its astonishing colours and glowing robes, its horses bedecked in silks and velvets with wonderfully decorated saddles and bridles. Everything was slightly worn out,

but glistening through all the dust was mica – a form of rock slivered like slate with the colourings of mother of pearl. Pressed into the damp mud of the newly faced walls, it gave a sequinned iridescence to all the public rooms of the palace.

The powerful images conjured up by living in this world of Arabian Nights was, for a child, like living on a huge film set. Perhaps this is why my attitude to interior design has always had a fantasy element about it.

Later, when I was a teenager, we moved to Lagos. After the arid scenery of the north, Lagos, with its 90 per-cent humidity,

(Opposite) All these designs are evolved from Mbari shrines. The normal earth colourings have been adapted to European taste. The lower illustration has been dealt with in two ways – the upper part was painted as normal and the lower part by using the wax-resist technique (page 128).

10

seemed like a different country. A strong seventeenth-century Portuguese influence could be seen there in the architecture which, with its brick-built houses painted and clad with fancy wrought-iron balconies and shutters, was most beautiful in a run-down sort of way. Not the quiet and order of the north, but a luscious overgrown jungle – noisy, laughing, colourful to the point of brashness, with everyone busy doing something to improve daily life, the kind of improvization one may not see anywhere else in the world, and always the big grin. Here, the hand painting of Adire cloth, dyed in indigo, is quite different from that of Kano, being mostly stencilled or painted using a feather or fine stick, rather than tied.

Throughout Nigeria, everything used in daily living was decorated, carved and often painted. These designs were traditional and all had an intrinsic meaning going back to time immemorial. Mud is usually chosen for its mystic properties of absorbing or repelling human radiation.

African mud sculpture which is practised in Nigeria is a living art, meaning that the art is created and then left to decay without protection or restoration. The designs are influenced by everyday life, and any new introductions such as cars, motorcycles or other modern equipment, tend to be reflected in what are their shrines. These works of art cannot be transported outside the forest areas so they are virtually unknown to Westerners.

These shrines, decorated with mud sculptures, are known as Mbari and can be found in the region of Owerri in the Ibo country.

The Mbari house, which is somewhat similar in feeling to a cloister, is built of large mud bricks, decorated on the outside face with holes, often glazed in European style. The rest of the building is decorated in earth colours of water-based paint, geometrically designed with patterns generations old, but which seemingly are placed at random. The life-sized and sometimes over-life-sized figures are placed with Ala – the Ibo goddess of earth – in the most prominent position. These figures are decorated in intricate patterns, some of them derived from Ibo body paintings, whilst others seem to be free variations.

Individual Influences

During my childhood, two months of every summer was spent in Devon and, for my fourteenth birthday, I was given private tuition in the techniques of oil painting. My teacher, Evelyn Street, was strict about cleanliness and the care of working tools so my first lessons were entirely taken up with brush maintenance and repair, including the re-setting of bent bristles with soap and rolling the damp brush in newspaper until it was dry. I was terrified of spilling paint on her expensive new studio matting but I have always been grateful for these lessons because I am now able to paint in almost any circumstances without fear of making marks on valuable objects. Years later, Evelyn told me that the matting had been laid specifically to teach us what she considered to be this most important lesson for our future.

Evelyn seldom instructed her pupils. She had a habit of 'leaving you to get on' and would just drop in now and then to criticize work or make her pupils solve their own mistakes. We had to think for ourselves and she would often say: 'I don't like to influence my pupils. Use your eyes, dear.' If anyone copied her style she was not at all flattered and would refuse to go on teaching them. Evelyn was the real start of my painting career and for the following two years all my free time was spent practising what I had learned from her.

In the year's gap between living in Kano and moving to Lagos, the family was sent off to New Zealand, where I attended Wellington art college every Saturday.

I was sixteen by the time we returned to Africa where I studied under one of Nigeria's most eminent artists, Erahbour Emokpae, who encouraged me to the point of suggesting my first exhibition at the age of seventeen. Much to my surprise it was a sell out.

However, in 1974, when I returned to England for good I did not find the subject matter inspiring and gave up painting to go into the antique trade. Years of dealing in antique art objects taught me to understand how to combine paint effects with period accuracy.

I didn't put paint to board until, some eleven years later, I was asked to design a kitchen shop, which involved choosing tiles for the displays. I was so appalled at the lack, in my opinion, of good design that it was suggested by my tenant-employer that I should start painting my own.

Thank goodness none of my friends was so truthful as to tell me how awful I was at first. Having got the bug, the paint brush never left my hand, and after some months I soon realized that I was improving all the time. Equally important, I discovered that instead of using oil paints, which took days to dry and cost a fortune, I could successfully achieve the results I wanted with emulsion and that it gave a far softer finish, which I call

My brother is in love with Brighton Pavilion and dragged me down to see it for the nth time, so I have dedicated this design to him. Although it decorates the hallways in the Pavilion, which are somewhat grander than most, it can enhance a rather austere room with its subtle colours and movement.

the 'falling apart palazzo look'. That air of decaying elegance, achieved so well by the Italians, fascinated me. All my holiday photographs of Italy that year were of peeling paintwork and damp-ridden walls. When I returned to England, I began to research in earnest how to reproduce this look and, as the pictures in this book demonstrate, it has taken over my life to a large degree.

New discoveries and methods crop up all the time and I test each one obsessively, often improving on an idea over several months or even years. I have also had lessons in Chinese methods of using brushes and paint which helps me technically when I am painting Chinese- or Japanese-style designs with bamboos etc.

Sense of Adventure

Having started in the antique trade with virtually no money, at first I could only afford to buy junk or total wrecks which had to be repaired. All this helped to give me a good grounding in the secret of furniture construction and design and, as business improved, better pieces were acquired, until the love of Queen Anne lacquer and Elizabethan oak seemed to dominate my buying trips. I soon found that you could buy these pieces if you were prepared to take on a pile of wood, instead of a set of chairs, or a chest covered in inches of paint, which had to be hand-stripped laboriously, coat by coat of paint and gook, so as not to risk spoiling the original patina underneath. This is really time consuming so many dealers will not touch a broken-up piece unless it is worth a mint. Still, it leaves the opportunity for us lowly types to make the best of a bad job, and often come out with something really worth all the effort.

Having slipped into the sixteenth-seventeenth centuries, I then found that it was not only furniture that had to be researched – I became infatuated with the look of that period, including curtain hanging cloth, gimps, floors, doors, furniture – in fact everything down to the last detail. Eventually this mania spread to the garden, which meant hours of research not only into contemporary design but also into which plants were used at that period.

In this book I have tried to explain my philosophy, my working techniques, my inspirations and to give an idea of the sort of interiors which can be achieved very easily with a little courage and a spirit of adventure. I hope you will enjoy the designs I have shown and may be encouraged to use or adapt them somewhere in your own home.

Part one:
Where it all Began

Paint Finishes

Once the technicalities have been perfected, many accidental paint effects will evolve by themselves. My attitude to painting is that you never stop learning or improving your control over brush or paint. This holds the interest of every artist, as they wonder what is around the corner or whether this will be the week when the longed-for perfection of any one object is finally achieved. The painted finish has been used for hundreds of years, changing in style and attitude with fashion, and the introduction of more modern methods in the production of paint has opened up the world of paint to us all. Now everyone can, with practice, accomplish whatever effect they desire on canvas or plaster.

This design was a complete departure from my normal colours. I tend to work a lot in blue but was persuaded to produce something quite new. Funnily enough, this design is now one of my favourites as I have a fantasy about it being used in a lovely old country house. The design is of a classical nature, the fruit and ribbons reminiscent of a Grinling Gibbons carving.

HELPFUL HISTORY

Walls

Among the earliest examples of walls decorated with 'paint' or powdered earth and charcoal were those of caves, on which the artists depicted hunting forays and scenes of everyday domestic life. Some of the first examples of 'interior decoration' came from Babylon and the wonderful creations in the Ancient Egyptian tombs which have influenced design throughout the centuries.

In the Middle Ages the Church was the greatest patron of the Arts, commissioning enormous murals and wall paintings, which were soon emulated by rich noblemen in their castles. As trade began to develop, objects of great value were brought back from far-off places, then copied by the local craftsmen, thus spreading new ideas throughout the known world.

Marbling was used as early as Egyptian and Roman times in house interiors, not because they could not afford the real stone, but because the effects could be painted in places where marble, being brittle and heavy, could not be used successfully.

Oil-based paint was already in use during the fifteenth century but many odd mixtures were used. Not all were successful, while others have lasted for centuries with little signs of deterioration. Binders and drying agents such as old egg white, glue size and various gums were employed to improve performance and quality.

Paint technology remained very primitive until a hundred years or so ago, all paint and stains being hand mixed by the artists. Each had to make do with whatever pigments were available locally and would keep his mixing methods highly secret so there was a huge variation in techniques. The colours in general use were somewhat limited. There were various reds: red lead, iron oxide, red ochre and vermilion-cinnabar; blues included woad, smalt and indigo; greens were verdigris and green earths; yellows were yellow ochre and lead-tin yellow; blacks were lamp black or bituminous earth. White lead was the normal cheap white.

Wood Panelling

Wood panelling was first used from around 1400 as an inner wall cladding to prevent draughts whistling through the cracks in stone and brickwork. At this stage it often reached ceiling height.

'Wainscot' or 'wagenshot' was the shipping term for a consignment of 'parcels' of wagon wood. From the Middle Ages large quantities of this wood were shipped as planks from the Baltic wharves to Britain and other European countries where it was used for building, furniture and panelling. The word 'clapboard' came into use around 1664, indicating smaller sizes of split oak, which were also imported. A panel is a square of plain or carved wood, held in position by a framework of wood known as rails (timbers running parallel to the floor) and stiles, known to me as uprights.

Only the wealthy could afford to use panels, often cladding an entire wall from floor to ceiling in oak. As time passed, the panels became heavily carved and often painted in bright geometric patterns.

During the sixteenth and seventeenth centuries, the linenfold design was carved into the panel, along with floral and geometric patterns – often the panels were inlaid with precious woods in stylized floral designs. The styles of panelling changed with the architecture and furniture fashions of the time.

Dados

Panelling dropped to dado height with the advent of tapestries introduced from Flanders and France. The original definition of a dado is the plinth of a column, hence the lower part of a wall, usually measuring around 3 feet (1 metre) in height.

In the seventeenth century an important function of the dado was to protect the wall-coverings which were often of silk and brocade. As the fashion was at that time to range chairs round the edge of the room, the dado protected the often priceless hangings from being marked by the chair backs. When interiors became more refined, panels were used as an integral part of the overall decoration and, by the eighteenth century, they were painted and carved in a more and more exotic fashion. Later, dado panelling was used less and all that was left was the dado rail. In modern times it is often only defined by the use of a different paint colour below the rail.

Panelled dados with fantasy wood graining were used in the hallways and on the banisters as a simple yet effective medium to show off my 'instant ancestors' to their best advantage. The use of strategically placed mirrors introduces light and space in rather restricted areas.

(Opposite) Originally a dark, hideous oak monstrosity, this fire surround was cut down by almost two-thirds all round to complement the proportions of my drawing room, and then painted to match the dados and borders. During the summer months it was the English tradition to place pleated paper fans into the grate as a simple yet formal decoration. (Right) Close-up showing the use of gold powders and stencil to create the acanthus leaf design which is much in evidence in Ham House, Richmond, Surrey.

(Overleaf, left) Persian pencil tree design from the Topkapi museum and (right) Magnolias in a Turkish vase with an acanthus leaf border.

The colour of early, unpainted panelling would have been rather similar to modern utility furniture and one would most certainly have disliked it intensely. But with smoke from open fires and constant beeswaxing, the colour became well toned down and, today, old panelling is the most beautiful mellow chestnut brown.

During the middle to late seventeenth century people began to paint the dado panelling in pastel shades with carved acanthus leaves, swags of fruit, birds and classical Palladian designs which were reflected in the highly decorated plasterwork. The carvings were either painted in deeper shades of the main colour or in contrasting colours and gilded.

Tiles

The British never wholeheartedly adopted the use of tiles on floors, unlike the French and Italians. But tiles had their place in millions of domestic fire surrounds and, with the introduction of transfers in the early nineteenth century, in public buildings as well. The fashion for blue and white tiles peaked during the eighteenth century and has held its own ever since.

The story really starts, centuries earlier, in China. The Islamic East had been importing Chinese porcelains from the eighth century and their local craftsmen had been copying the Chinese designs during all that time. Marco Polo spent seventeen years with the Kublai Khan, obviously bringing home samples with him and, in 1416, we see the first evidence of this in the inventory of the Duc du Berry's estate, which contained entries of porcelain china. What had started as merely a slow trickle of imported porcelain from the Far East in the fourteenth century, including blue and white, was to change by the sixteenth century into a flood of wonderful examples including Famille Verte and Famille Rose.

The blue of Chinese blue and white was cobalt oxide, covered with transparent glaze, the colour becoming an intense blue when it was fired at a temperature of 1280°C. In fact, the Chinese had intended to produce a black glaze. When the result turned out to be blue, they exported it anyway and the blue and white became all the rage in Europe.

In 1715 the British East India Company became the first established company in Canton. The Dutch followed in 1729. By this time traders throughout Europe were fighting to be importers of porcelain, textiles and Chinese lacquered panels.

Factories were springing up all over the place. Delft, Liverpool, Bristol and Lambeth were the largest producers of polychrome and blue and white. The whole interior look of the West was undergoing an immense change from dour oak, stark stone and heavily tapestried walls to the gleaming silks, lacquers, gilding and paintings inspired by the East. Can't you imagine the yellows, blacks, blues and whites of ceramics and silks, jostling each other for pride of place in the, by now, more spacious and airy rooms of sophisticated Europeans?

21

(Opposite) This column was made for me in lieu of rent by a hard-up tenant. I love columns; they can play a significant part in lending an aura of grandeur to any dull area. Columns can be used for statuary, plants, wonderful flower arrangements or, in fact, anything worthy of display. This rather unusual colourway of sea blue and terracotta seems to lend itself to most surroundings.

(Overleaf) This seventeenth-century bedroom is totally overtaken by the bed. I treated the original pine wood to look like oak. Because of the bed's size, one is forced to sidle from one side of the room to the other! The bed hangings I embroidered on to antique velvet curtains, using silver and gold bullion thread. The walls are very washed, blue, battered French. Although the Chinese lacquer mirror could have proved too sophisticated for the room it, in fact, fits in beautifully.

Furniture

Brightly painted furniture was fashionable in Britain as far back as the 1550s and is still popular in many countries. In fact the Tudors painted their oak furniture in geometric designs, not only to protect the wood, but, I would imagine, to add colour and light to their sometimes rather dreary houses. During the early seventeenth century furniture was painted to simulate marble and wood panelling and there are many examples still in existence today.

Graining was another method used to make cheap woods look more costly. The technique was adopted in England towards the end of the sixteenth century. Of course today there are few examples left of this painted furniture as, over the years, with polish and general wear and tear, the paint has either faded or become chipped, and the piece discarded by the ever fashion-conscious English, often to the servants' quarters.

If paints have been popular over the years, so have stains. The difference between them is that paint is opaque and usually used on stone, plaster, wood and other hard surfaces, whereas stain is translucent, penetrating wood and leaving the grain to show through, rather than covering the surface. Coloured stains were often used to dye cloth, such as hangings, flags or banners.

The high fashion for painted furniture waned towards the second half of the sixteenth century, as the craze for the oriental lacquered finish took its place, but the painting of furniture returned to general use in the late eighteenth century, having its ups and downs in popularity until this day.

With the opening up of the Orient, via the new trade routes, japanned or lacquered panels were imported into Europe. True lacquer was made from the sap of the *Rhus vernicifera*, commonly known as the 'Lac-tree'. When done properly, the solution is applied in thin layers on to a basket work base or later on to soft wood. This process is extremely long-winded but one of the most durable applied finishes ever used by man – to the extent that, if made thick enough, it can be carved in high relief. Later, the English and Dutch developed their own methods of simulating japanning with varnishes and gums, and lacquering superseded the paint finish until the early eighteenth century.

It could be said that this rebirth in fashion of painted furniture was due to Robert Adam, as furniture formed an essential part of his comprehensive decorative schemes, setting off the classical architectural style of that time. The difference between the earlier painted furniture and that of the eighteenth century was that the former had been painted in mostly primary colours, giving a primitive look, whereas Adam and his followers tended to use light colours in pastel shades, often applying paint on a polished wood surface in the form of medallions and flowered swags. These designs still influence the painted finish of today, having been used time and again as this form of painting came back into vogue.

Textiles

Coarse linen and hemp, painted in oils and stains, usually depicting biblical and mytho-logical scenes along with more general subjects were used by all classes throughout the sixteenth century. The bed hangings and curtains in the court of Elizabeth I and in the nobles' houses had applied decoration either in paint or stain, depicting flowers, birds, insects, humans and animals, with mag-nificent crowned roses and fleur-de-lis pat-terns. Such painted cloth was mentioned in wills, along with prized furniture, and if the owner moved house, would be taken down and carefully refitted in the new home.

It was not until the East India Company established itself in Surat, India, that large amounts of cloth with new designs were brought to Europe. Surat was the main tex-tile port in the early seventeenth century along with Ahmedabad, which was also a centre for gold thread known as bullion, used in vast quantities throughout the East and Europe. The trade peaked between the six-teenth and seventeenth centuries and in fact still goes on today but in a very minor way.

At first, the English imported painted palampores to use as bedcovers. These were lengths of cloth with strong-coloured back-grounds and white designs of Indian or Persian-style flowers and leaves. This proved a disastrous failure since the British were disappointed at the lack of colour, so the importers decided to reverse the pattern (i.e. give it a white background and coloured flowers and trees). This time the British did not like the crude motifs and still would not buy the cloth, so the shippers took samples of designs and drawn-up palampores out to Surat to start factories reproducing English designs on local cloths. This was an out-standing success. The British went mad over the new colours, but unfortunately they were rather slow in getting their ideas to Surat on a regular basis, so the French and Dutch even-tually cornered the market.

25

To prepare a palampore correctly, twenty-six stages were involved before the actual pattern could be painted on to the cloth. The designs being sent over to Surat were from a totally different culture. The Indians had never seen the birds, animals and insects portrayed, and certainly not the English oak. In the enlarging process, which always changes the finer points of a pattern, our famous English oak leaf and all the 'foreign' motifs became distorted.

The invading Moghul Empire was not too enthusiastic about Indian style either, and, like the English found it rather crude, so they imported Persian miniature painters to their courts, who ended up presenting a mixture of the finer Indian designs mixed with Persian. Many of the small motifs used in Indian art were in turn influenced by Islamic art. So were born the crewel work designs used in the embroidery of hangings in England during the second half of the seventeenth century (see page 38). Thus the borrowing and adapting of designs has an ancient and honourable tradition!

THE CONTEMPORARY VISION

The fashion for the painted effect seems never totally to have waned, often declining in popularity but always coming back to blossom somewhere. Luckily, there are many books and examples which survive from earlier times, giving us the basis for our work of today. Although some of us may not wish to follow these examples to the letter, it is good to have the chance to refer to these past recipes and to masters of the art.

The Importance of Research

I have found the easiest way to research, apart from looking at hundreds of books and magazines, and any literature you can lay your hands on, is in fact to traipse round all the houses open to the public of your chosen period, often visiting the same set of houses time and time again, as you extend your interest from one feature of the house to the other. Ham House, near Richmond in Surrey, Cotehele House in Cornwall and Montacute House in Somerset are particular favourites of mine. Take the time to wander round the garden as well, since this is really an extension of the home. The idea is to get an impression of the total effect.

When I first started dealing in furniture I was drawn towards the sixteenth and seventeenth centuries very quickly. I spent hours looking through books on the architecture of the period. Having chosen your period, look at contemporary paintings, as they can' be very useful sources of interior styles. Museums can be helpful with fabric and textile designs as well as furniture and chinaware, and even tiles, which may not always be illustrated in books. A good source of information is your local antique shop. Antique dealers really will not mind you wandering around, looking and asking questions. Such visits also give an idea of prices and whether you will be able to afford the real thing. Sale rooms are another source of great interest as you will spy all sorts of things which may not necessarily be of the correct period but good enough copies so that they can be altered to fit your desired effect once painted.

Whatever style you choose, research is vitally important because a style is made up of so many different components. You will probably find you get a bee in your bonnet about one subject at a time. For a few months you will be fascinated by all sorts of textiles; curtains, hangings, fabrics and upholstery and then suddenly you will want to know all about doors, handles, window frames etc instead. Soon you will have covered the entire house and its secret ways of establishing a certain style.

All this research may sound laborious and expensive, but really it is not. On the contrary, once you realize that you can neither find nor afford the real chair or painting of the period, it is fun and satisfying to use a nineteenth-century copy, of which there are plenty available. Re-upholstered in suitable fabric, it will be transformed. Second-hand cloth can result in a very close approximation to the original antique.

I find this more exciting than unearthing an antique of my desired period, which I generally cannot afford, so derive hours of pleasure from browsing in antique and second-hand shops, and finding the longed-for tassel or stool which I can bring to life with paint. While researching, be prepared to put up with quantities of papers and re-

---

My mother returned from a visit to the West Indies and asked me to make up a mirror design she had seen out there. This is a three-way mirror which hangs on the wall; when not in use it looks like a painting and opens out for use. The George III table underneath was brought in for restoration by Lord Rendlesham who is an antique dealer client of mine.

search material all over the floors and tables of your home (which drives the other occupants of the household insane). Copious notes, sketches and examples usually end up in some carrier bag, to be hauled from place to place. Make sure you choose plastic, unlike my mother, who often drops the whole lot, and who was once seen surrounded by fluttering papers, as figures darted back and forth across an airport runway, trying to retrieve them.

Achieving the Style

The following pages illustrate a number of rooms which I have designed. You may like to start by doing something similar or simply use them as inspirational ideas for schemes of your own.

I am happy that the dado in purely decorative form is back. Dados play a large part in my ideas for decoration and can have varying optical illusions, making a small room appear larger, or a room with nooks and crannies, jutting walls and a sunken floor, more unified. I have also discovered that when doing my battered French technique (see page 64) that the space left between dado and ceiling becomes more manageable. A dado can provide a pleasing break in vast expanses of wall and help the not-so-grand to appear more interesting.

Thornton's Panelled Dining Room

A good example of how I work can be seen in the panelling I did for a client. She wanted her dining room painted in a similar style to the Monet house at Giverny, just outside Paris, which has wonderful sunny yellow walls. She owned a set of china in blue and yellow and so I decided to paint the walls in a simple panel design using the same blue and yellow.

The upper walls were painted in battered French (see page 64) in a soft, light shade of yellow, with darkish blue squares to simulate painted panels, leaving out the shading as the whole room was to look painted and simple. Below the dado I used a darker shade of the same yellow, with the same blue for the lower panelling. To make the room appear larger, the doors were treated in the same manner as the rest of the wall area. The bookcase, which was built by my cabinet maker, was painted yellow with blue stringing on the edge of the shelves to give it extra importance.

Stringing is a term used in the antique trade for a line of inlaid wood or other matierial used to contrast with surrounding veneers.

I used blue paint to get a similar effect. I adjusted the panel sizes so they fitted elegantly into the wall space, taking into account my client's lovely and important collection of paintings, which should be shown off to their best advantage. The panel lines were then hand-painted because I find masking tape time-consuming to put up and because, if not properly pressed down at the edges with a knife, it is liable to make the paint bleed. Then when you lift it off, half the wall comes away with it. All in all, it is easier to practise painting straight lines.

I have found the best method is to paint the two edges first, as you only have to think about keeping one side of the line perfect, then fill in the middle.

This dining room was commissioned by one of the partners of the Redfern Gallery who loved Monet's house at Giverny. It perfectly complemented her collection of contemporary paintings, so was deliberately kept as simple as possible, the clear yellows lending light to a dark basement area.

This tiny bedroom in a Chelsea London town house received a similar treatment to the dining room opposite, but was feminised with the introduction of Empire swags and sprigs in Adam greens and pinks to offset the period bed, which I painted with my client's favourite flowers of columbines and roses.

Georgian Panelled Bedroom

Another client, seeing the dining room described above, loved it so much that she asked if I could do something similar, but with a little more to it than just plain lining, as it was for a bedroom which she wanted to look classical but feminine.

I chose to add the swags of leaves at the top of each panel because the decoration of this room was so plain and simple. I repeated the running leaf design at the top of the room, just below the cornice and on the dado line under the main panels to give the room unity. I painted smaller panels on the dado with a sprig of leaves gathered with a ribbon in the centre of each.

The colours were dictated by the curtains and bed already in the room, so although the green may look different at first glance from the material, it is actually mixed to match part of the shading on the leaves.

Both the client and I were amazed at the visual transformation of a room which by many standards is rather small. It looked much larger and took on an air of 'petite grandeur'.

You will note that neither of these rooms uses my antiquing methods. Neither client wanted this aged effect, preferring a fresh look, so the colours were mixed to appear soft.

Variations on a Theme of Tulips

The tulip design has been used for hundreds of years on tiles, cloth and china. Tulips were originally imported from Turkey, where they grew wild. During the sixteenth century they became popular in Holland, Belgium and England, rising to a sort of frenzied fame during the early seventeenth century, when whole fortunes were made and lost through speculation in tulip bulbs. Through the years, tulips have become a common sight in our gardens and are still loved and used as an inspiration by designers today.

These three tulip designs were painted to show how a favourite motif can be trans-formed to look quite different in various settings.

I designed the baskets of fruit with ribbons with the idea of using this pattern in a large country house, in the dining room, kitchen or passageways. The light pinks and yellow ochres seem to have that softness a country house requires, echoing the orchard fruits one would expect to come across during the summer and early autumn. I felt that with worn, painted furniture or light fruit wood and marble or stone floors, this rather quiet yet sophisticated design would melt into the emptiness that old houses seem to harbour during cool afternoons of an English summer, when it is usually pelting with rain.

The exotic shape of the tulip lends itself to many designs. If you are a fanatic about this flower, as I am, you may want to use it in more than one room of the house. This forced me to create a series of variations on a similar theme and I thought it would be of interest to show (left and right) how one design could be reworked time and time again.

German Secretaire

This German secretaire has had a long and motley career in my family. I have always loved large, exotic pieces of furniture and when I found this magnificent piece on my travels to Lincolnshire, I overcame my shyness at spending three times my standard price (£50 at the time) for any one item. My family and friends, horrified, said 'What do you want that monstrosity for?'

It was the height of the pine-stripping craze and for some years my pride and joy remained stripped with walnut panels. I had no room for it so it passed from one member of the family to another until finally it came full circle back to me, this time to be painted.

I decided to leave the highly decorative panels in their original state but painted the pine part in two coats of strong red terracotta to obscure the natural wood underneath. When they were dry I sponged on a dark, thick brown paint with overtones of red. Before this dried, I took a clean, damp sponge and highlighted all the carved areas and the areas where it would become more worn, letting the terracotta show through. I finished off the whole with several coats of beeswax polish. The scratches have appeared through constant use and, in my opinion, add to the lived-in look.

One of my more extravagant buys, which created a family argument, was this German secretaire. These detailed shots are to show how simulated wear and tear can be effected when restoring old pieces of furniture.

Japanese Bamboo

Japanese Bamboo (page 116) took years to perfect. It was one of those things I couldn't master. But one day when I was all set to paint the Chinese magnolias and bamboo (page 124), I just could not resist another try on that glorious yellow and it worked. This time I had discovered the trick – I could paint in a similar fashion to the Japanese.

Oh! the excitement. Now all that remains is to find the house to use it in. The main idea was taken from Edo period Japanese screens with a few variations of my own. These screens look simple and that's precisely their difficulty. The contrived balance of the simplified plants and trees is so perfect that it is impossible for a Westerner to arrive at the same elegance without it looking overworked and studied.

The Japanese version of bamboo, as illustrated here, is far stronger in its statement than the Chinese, thus allowing you to use it in larger spaces less filled with ornaments.

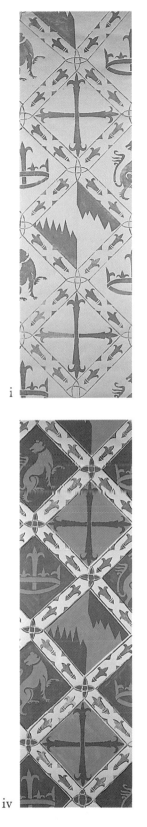

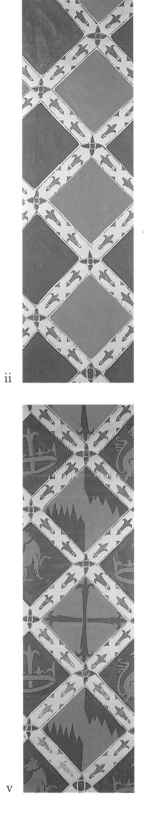

i

ii

iii

iv

v

Here are five different stages of a design. Having cut the stencil for the basic design, it soon becomes apparent that you can actually do as much or as little as the whim takes you. This is unusual in that, with most designs, you will find that a particular colourway will look best but here you can rework the colours at different stages and add the final stages to your own taste. The Heraldic devices can be omitted or changed for your own favourite motif.

How Lazy Do You Feel?

This design was influenced by a Florentine wall of the fourteenth or fifteenth century. Having researched the design and cut the stencils for the downstairs hall, in the end I never used it and this is the first time it has seen the light of day. I thought it would be interesting to experiment with the various different ways that it could be used and soon realized that it was one of those rare occasions when a pattern seemed to work in at least five ways by adding a bit here and there to the basic stencil design. In fact, I could have gone on developing the different stages using the same colourway ad infinitum. As you can see, each stage is a progression of the preceding one and you can go on as long as you are interested or stop when it becomes boring.

Tree of Life

You will see this cropping up throughout the book in one form or another. It is, of course, a direct result of the crewel work designs used on the bed hangings in the seventeenth century. First of all, I hung two beds with the embroidery and, having got to know the design so well, I felt it had potential used on walls, as I was not about to sit down and sew hundreds of feet of Irish linen to achieve the effect! The Tree of Life is a boldly drawn design, worked as a rule in dark blues and greens with a small amount of brown, consisting of leafy stems, generally serpentine in form, rising from a base of hilly ground and with the added diversity of small animals. In early examples, a definite influence can be traced to the hand-drawn and painted cloths and palampores from Surat and Masulipatnam in India. Crewel work is peculiar to England, not being done anywhere else in the world. Later hangings, made at the end of the century, were worked in lighter colours. It occurred to me that not everyone might want to have the whole design over their walls so I decided to transfer this embroidery idea to the dado, leaving you the choice of using it in tapestry form or just as a dado.

This design evolved when I was doing crewel work embroidery and I then transferred variations on to other surfaces: walls first, then tiles and finally a kitchen work surface. Although the design is fairly intricate, it is really quite quick to do and can be repeated without noticeably using the same forms, therefore appearing freehand.

Chinese Plate

This was inspired by a much treasured Mason's Ironstone plate given to me (after some persuasion) by an antique dealer. It is badly broken and clumsily glued together but has the most glorious colours, mixing spindleberries with peonies – two of my favourite flowers. I did the design specifically for this book to show how a design can evolve from any source.

People love this cracked plate, one of my treasured items, so I decided to design a simple dado and border from it (below). This treatment could, of course, be applied to any favoured china, changing the design just enough not to be an exact copy.

Two Chinese Style Dining Rooms

The taste for decorating in the Chinese style was at its height of fashion in the eighteenth century, having been introduced to England by Sir William Chambers who sailed on a Swedish vessel to China in 1748–9, bringing home drawings of Chinese decorations, paintings and furniture. Shortly afterwards, in 1754, Edwards and Darly issued a book on Chinese designs, thus popularizing the style.

Many years ago I was asked to help restore some Queen Anne Chinese hand-painted wallpaper but, unfortunately, my client ran out of money so the restoration was never done.

However, I had already started to research Chinese techniques for reproducing the style which was used for this paper. My lessons in Chinese methods of brush control and paint were a great help technically for this design. Over the years I have evolved a method of using stencils for the basic design and then

The English have a curious affinity with China. English gardens often contain masses of Chinese plants such as peonies, poppies and chrysanthemums which inspire some of my paintings and designs. Here I have used my clients' favourite plants, which they wanted depicted on their dining room walls. Since the room had four doors, these had to be hidden by painting the frieze without interruption.

40

This room was painted after the example opposite, again to the client's special requirements. My idea was to make each dining room appear as individual as possible, so the door and dado was dragged and marbled, giving a darker but more architectural look, to which the room lent itself as it had higher ceilings.

over-painting veins, stems and flower details afterwards so the whole effect is half-stencil, half-painted.

Both these rooms were decorated within weeks of each other because the second client had seen the first room and liked it. The problem was that both lived in the same street so that I could not paint an exact replica. On the other hand, to sit down and cut totally new stencils seemed rather expensive for the client so I compromised and cut half new ones, making sure I did not use the first client's favourite trees for the second client. The fact that both rooms were basements made things even more difficult. In the end I decided to treat the doors and dados in a completely different manner on each project.

This was one of my first experiences of making one design idea look totally different and, in fact, it was not as difficult as I had at first thought. Both clients told me confidentially that they preferred their own dining room.

Discussion on Paint

Water-based paints in the form of emulsions, gouache and powder colours are this book's main theme. I use them because they are clean to handle, making maintenance of brushes and sponges easier; quicker to dry, enabling you to do several coats within hours; and, above all because they give me the visual effect I need when recreating the chalky, aged look of distemper without all the washing off and flaking that true lime created in the old days. The colour difference between water-based paints and oils is pronounced. The light catches on the shine of oil paint, making it brighter and harder to the eye than the softer, subtle effects achievable with water-based paint.

This image was created in the style of a seventeenth-century still life painting, bringing together all the implements which I currently use. I have been most fortunate in that my mother goes 'brush hunting' on her visits to China, presenting me with these magnificent examples as welcome gifts on her return.

Why I Use Water-based Paints

When decorating an interior, paint plays a very important part in harmonizing the overall effect and is a cheap way of covering a wall.

This book is about decorating with water-based paints. There is a very great difference between the effect of oil and water-based paints and nearly all the recipes I use are for emulsions. I have developed the habit of doing all the paint work in emulsion – windows, doors, even radiators – and have found that it wears just as well if treated with respect. Equipment, if well kept should not become hardened or clogged with use. Some of the equipment can be raided from the kitchen: bowls, saucers and spatulas, for instance. (You can then wash them up in time for the next meal!) Brushes, however, are a different matter and can cost a minor fortune, which is why it's important to maintain them.

Oil paints are brighter and harder in tone, perhaps because they reflect more light off their shiny surfaces and, when used for sponging, oil paints tend to leave masses of little pointed deposits on the wall which catch the light in an ugly manner. Emulsions and other water-based paints are flat and so absorb the light. Emulsions are quicker to dry and therefore avoid the boring time spent waiting to get the next coat on. They are also cleaner to use unless you want to spend your whole life with your hands dipped in white spirit.

In my opinion, it is not necessary to glaze or seal any of the water-based paint finishes, although you must do so in areas which might suffer water penetration. My experience is they tend to last longer and are easier to re-touch if they remain unsealed. If you must seal a surface, always use a matt glaze. But remember that a sealant will change the colour of the paint finish over a period of time.

Finally, when it is time to repaint the room completely, there is no need to sand off the old paint (a job I truly hate). With water-based paints you can simply wash the wall and then paint directly on to the old finish.

The only time I use oil-based paints is very occasionally as an undercoat in places where water might get in, such as bathrooms and kitchens, or on something like cast iron where oil paint is more likely to inhibit rust. If you use oil-based undercoat you can use artists' oils when mixing a colour.

The main disadvantage of water-based paint is that you have to be very quick, as the drying time is drastically decreased, especially if you have central heating or it is high summer – not much risk of that in England. If you drop a teaspoon of glycerine into about 1 pint (½ litre) of the paint mix, it should prolong the drying out. Add more if it's still drying too quickly.

Another definite minus is that it is not easy to rectify mistakes when using techniques like battered French. Your only option is to start that wall again from scratch, if you cannot live with the mistake you've made, or cover it up with a mirror as I once had to do. Techniques such as marbling and sponging can be rectified without too much difficulty. Perhaps this is why I have evolved my antiquing methods to such perfection, as one more bash does not look so bad when the walls and skirtings are not totally perfect in the first place.

With two dogs and their friends and a cat in the house as well as myself, constantly painting and moving furniture around, my walls have survived remarkably well.

Mixing Paint

I basically use white emulsion paint. Emulsion paints come ready to use, except for the colour variations you want to achieve, which are done by mixing pigments into the paint.

I sometimes use pure pigments but these can cause you tremendous problems. Add too much pigment and you run the risk that the paint will not dry. Unless you have experience of using these products, and it has taken me many years to get the quantities right, I suggest you use the alternative ways of mixing colours. Both gouache and powder paint are comparatively easy to mix and very effective.

Gouache is paint in which the opaque powder pigments are already mixed in water (and traditionally thickened with gum and honey).

Powder paints (like the powder paints used for painting at school) are bought in tins and must be mixed with water.

When using gouache or powder paint on its own, mix a little emulsion into the colour to stabilize the paint.

It may be of great benefit to spend some time just playing around with mixing all sorts of colours; you will surprise yourself, and will no doubt come up with different shades you never dreamed possible. It is fun and worth the trouble as it will acquaint you with the do's and don'ts of paint mixtures. It may also be of interest since it will take you some time to be able to judge the quantities of paint needed for any one job. It is always wise to mix more than you think you will need, because, although you may measure really carefully, the next paint mix will be slightly different. Any excess can be stored for further use. I never throw any paint away; either it is remixed or used again.

Light hits each wall surface in a different way, automatically changing the colour, and the same can be said for furniture. If you find that you have run out of paint, mix up the nearest match possible and start from a new edge. In a room, start on the next corner. If you have run out in the middle of the wall you will have to do that wall again so it is better not to start if you feel that you haven't enough of the original paint to finish one whole wall. The same goes for a piece of furniture, although you will probably never run into this problem as you are not dealing with such large surfaces. Also, on a piece of furniture you will not be able to deceive the eye so easily.

All water paints can be mixed so that they are quite thick or very runny, almost to the consistency of water. A cream-like consistency is what you need for most techniques. But if you are mixing paint to add an antiqued look, it must be very thin indeed, and quite muddy in colour – I call it 'dirty dishwater'. If you have any difficulty mixing the paint, for instance if it goes lumpy or has formed a skin, you can pass it through an ordinary large kitchen sieve. (A sieve with a pointed base will fit almost any receptacle.) Use a wooden spatula to ease the paint through the sieve holes. Remember to wash the sieve immediately after use or the holes will get blocked up.

I wanted to show this corner of one of the Chinese style dining rooms so that you would be able to see how the light changes from one wall face to another, thus alleviating the worry of running short of paint. The other point to note is that the stencils can be carried round corners without any problem.

45

Brushes for Water-based Paint Finishes

You will need a number of brushes, preferably several of each size and type. *Always* buy the best. Some of these brushes are expensive but it makes all the difference in the world if you use real sable or squirrel hair rather than a substitute. I have paid as much as £60 for a brush and not regretted it.

KEY FOR PAGE 43: 1 badger hair flogger; 2 squirrel fan; 3 badger hair fan brush; 4 uncut goose feather; 5 cut goose feather; 6 squirrel mop; 7 liner; 8–10 pencil sable hairs; 11, 12 and 14, 15 Chinese calligraphy brushes; 13 2″ (5cm) Chinese calligraphy brush; 16, 17 3-pronged and 7-pronged pipe-over brushes; 18 charcoal holder; 19 1″ (2.5cm) fitch; 20 ½″ (1.5cm) fitch; 21 ¼″ (1cm) fitch; 22 1″ (2.5cm) varnish brush; 23 3″ (7.5cm) varnish brush

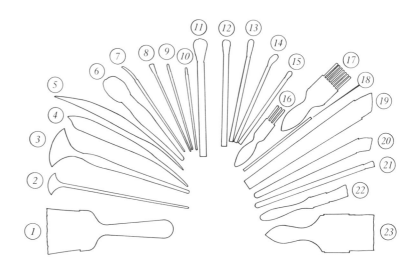

The most useful brushes I have found are:

* 4 good-quality paint brushes ranging in width from 1in (2.5cm) to 4in (10cm)
* 2 fitches, ½in (1.5cm) and 1in (2.5cm). These are made of hog's or pole cat's hair
* 3 sable pencil brushes, nos. 2 to 4
* 2 squirrel fan brushes, no. 2 and no. 5. This is a fan brush which looks like a fan
* 1 squirrel mop brush, shaped like the end of a fox's tail or a washing-up mop
* 1 badger softener (optional)
* A range of Chinese calligraphy brushes
* 1 pipe-over brush. This is a flat brush with three or seven metal tubes set into the ferrule, each with tufts of hair coming out of the end of the tubes, which is used for graining. I also used it for the ploughed-field effect in the Tree of Life design.

If you cannot afford to buy a badger softener, you can get a similar effect with any good household brush if you soak it in water for forty-eight hours then bash it with a hammer while it is still wet to split the hairs and soften it. Badger softeners or 'floggers' can be used for blending and softening colours when marbling, although I personally use a damp, natural sponge.

When you begin work, your brush should always be clean and dry with straight bristles. Make sure you have a bucket of clean water at hand and leave the brush in the water so that it doesn't harden during use. Always clean brushes in lukewarm water after a painting session. First, squeeze concentrated washing-up liquid into a small bowl or the palm of your hand, and work the brush backwards and forwards until it is completely free of paint, and then rinse it thoroughly, several times, until the water runs clear. Lay out all the brushes to dry on a length of old towelling. If a brush has been left to dry and the bristles are crooked, pass the brush over a tablet of soap on both sides. Roll the brush in newspaper, ensuring the bristles are straight, and fold the paper over just the end of the bristles. Secure with an elastic band and leave for twenty-four hours to dry. Rinse before use.

Never leave brushes to dry with their bristles in the air, as this rots the ferrule.

I always use more than one brush of each size and several sponges as it is unwise to paint with a soggy brush: no matter how well you think you have drained it, some water always remains in the ferrule which dribbles, if not all over your hands then down the wall, leaving a ghastly mess and ruining hours of hard work. Before you finish at night, clean and lay out your brushes so that you can start with properly dry ones in the morning. If, by any chance, you are forced to use a soggy brush, take the precaution of wrapping kitchen paper round the ferrule to catch the drips.

Working with Water-based Paints

Always protect furniture and floors with dustsheets.

Some people might advise finishing off with a coat of varnish or polyurethane. In my opinion varnishing changes the colour of the paint. In fact, I have seen a room alter completely even where a special varnish was used whose instructions said this would not happen. Another reason is that paint on radiators or woodwork chips far more easily when sealed. And, unless you are a wizard with a brush, you will always miss bits out and after a time the unsealed areas oxidize – usually going darker – so that every time you walk past you are reminded that there is a spot you missed. Too irritating for words, as you do not need to be reminded day in and day out that you are less than perfect – and it's there for all the world to see.

On the practical side, when the decorating is finished, walls and woodwork get grubby with fingermarks. A gentle rub with a damp cloth and a small amount of washing-up liquid will usually remove any grease marks without pulling half the paint away.

When the paint is dry, I treat window sills with a spray-on polish to make dusting easier. I spray the polish on to a soft, clean cloth (curtain interlining is excellent), and wipe over the surface I want to protect. If sills are given this treatment, it will stop the duster from snagging on any slightly rough areas.

Colour

Colour is a very individual thing. I may call a blue 'pale blue' and another person will say it is 'duck egg blue'. I now very rarely discuss the colour of a paint, as either I am colour blind or the next person sees a different colour to me.

Use the colours that you like and forget about the rules. For instance, in a north-facing room which tends to have a hard, cool light, I might use a pale colour to give the room a more sunny appearance. Many people use shades of white or pastel tones to help lighten a dark room, but it's not necessary. I really think that if the room is dark and you wish to use dark colours, you should do so. Pale colours may, in fact, *not* lighten the room and could draw attention to its lack of light.

Another old wives' tale is that blue should only be used in bathrooms. Certainly it is not a warm or sunny colour, and many people consider it cold. I personally cannot agree. Almost any colour can appear impersonal and cool if not treated in the correct manner. I love all the blue shades from pale to dark and use them constantly, as you will see looking through the book.

After years of experience it is possible to look at a colour and analyze the different pigments of primary colours that have been mixed together to produce a certain shade. In order to help those who have not had this experience, I have given a colour chart opposite which has been constructed to help take the mystery out of mixing your paint.

Pigments were usually made by grinding down earths, clays and semi-precious stones in a pestle and mortar and mixing the pure colour with stabilizers. I always keep a supply of earth colours and add them to a paint colour when I want a dull and aged paint mix. These are the ones I keep:

This room is long and narrow with rather high windows and dark, heavy furniture, so I kept the walls very plain, using a warm stone colour on top with a terracotta, faded marble effect on the dados.

Raw umber	brown red-purple
Burnt umber	deep brown red-purple
Raw sienna	light yellow-brown red-purple
Burnt sienna	deep brown-red, red-purple
French yellow ochre	yellow red-purple
Lampblack	black blue

To obtain a good Prussian blue which is very dark, add black to cobalt or ultramarine.

This could go on forever, and it would only become confusing, so I really suggest that the best method is to keep practising.

Colour Mixes I Constantly Use	
Terracotta	red or Indian red chrome yellow small quantity of yellow ochre white touch of black
'French green'	blue cobalt or ultramarine yellow ochre small quantity of black white
Grey	black and white *Add small quantity of* yellow ochre or ultramarine blue or red
Yellow ochre	yellow ochre small quantity of black white
Pink	red or crimson lake white black yellow ochre
Red (as in the German secretaire on page 34)	bright red chrome yellow touch of black
Malachite green	chrome yellow ultramarine viridian green
Very dark green	viridian green black
Dark brown	black red touch of yellow ochre

Throughout this book I suggest adding a touch of black or brown to take the edge off a colour. Any of the earth colours can be used for this as well and you will soon learn to adapt to your own mixtures. I have intentionally not gone into much detail on colour mixing, since it is only by practice and experience that you will get the particular colours you want.

Simple Colour Mixes

My aunt always said that you should never use pure white on walls or furniture. Always drop into the white one of the following: red, yellow ochre, black or blue, perhaps a dessertspoon to a gallon or 10ml to a 5-litre pot. To the naked eye this might not appear to make any difference but, in fact, when the paint is applied in any quantity you will see a slight glow from the added colour.

When mixing primary colours into larger quantities of white paint, which I always use as a base, do so little by little. I put a mugful of the base white into a basin and add the colours, slowly, stirring all the time with a wooden spatula. When the colours are completely blended, I add more of the white paint, in all about four mugfuls.

The mixture is now ready to transfer into the main body of paint. Keep stirring until it is perfectly blended.

When mixing grey, I usually use black and white but introduce a tiny quantity of one of the colours mentioned above to soften the harshness of the black.

When adding yellow ochre to black and white, take care that it does not turn green. A squashed caterpillar green is obtained from yellow ochre and black mixed. (This may not be the colour you wanted, but it can come in useful sometimes.)

Red, when added to black will produce mauve, another colour mix to be careful about.

Texture

I am often asked to paint all sorts of objects to disguise them, such as cast iron painted as stone or terracotta, or vice versa. The urn on page 50 is cast iron. I used oil-based paint to help stop the rust, whilst achieving a stone finish to match the concrete base.

It is important with textured finishes that you get a sense of depth. This can be done by

(Overleaf, left) This garden is a tiny London courtyard which is wonderfully overgrown, at once giving that secret garden feeling and hiding thirty-foot high walls of uninterrupted London bricks. Rather than painting the cast iron urns the usual white or black, I was requested to apply a stone effect so that one could discover the garden statuary peeping out amongst highly scented trailing roses, honeysuckle and grapevines. This visual image leads one to suppose that the garden goes on round the next corner which, of course, it does not. (Right) The fireplace, as described in the text, is another one of my money-saving ventures, using cement instead of stone.

applying several layers of very thin paint. The more shades you add, overlapping one colour on another, the more depth the finish will have.

The stone effect can be used to save loads of money when replacing a fire surround. Having bought an oak fire surround, I should have had stone slips made to fit on the inner side of the wooden frame, in order to prevent the wood from getting too hot and perhaps igniting. As usually happens, money was rapidly getting used up on all the little extras that one never allows for, so it was cement and paint that saved the day. After much trouble, I managed to explain to my builder exactly how the cement should look when finished. In reality, the surrounds should be made up of three separate pieces of stone, with chamfered inner edges. Since he obviously thought me quite mad and did not understand what I meant by chamfered edges, we had to make a trip up and down the street peering at everybody's window surrounds until I came across the exact example of what was required. While the cement rendering was still 'green', the chamfered edges were cut in and two lines marked out to simulate where the stone joints would have been. After it was finished, the man stepped back to admire his clever handiwork as if it was all his own invention.

Once the cement had dried off I chose to use a sandstone colour which is more yellow in hue than granite or purbeck. The fireplace, now complete, was inspected by a client, who was furious to think that she had just spent six times as much as myself on the real thing only to have a slightly better finish. In fact, she liked my coloration better than her stone, which tends to the cooler grey side. This, I thought cheerfully, is what lack of money can achieve for you.

Painting wood to look like wood may seem to be the most ridiculous idea if you do not intend to do some marvellous graining, but in fact, having spent fourteen years dyeing, staining and bleaching wood to either match or age it, one becomes somewhat sick of this very tedious long-winded operation and longs for a slapdash, quick method to present itself. So one day, feeling tired and as usual running against the clock, because the house seems to be under constant inspection from someone or another, I quickly slapped some paint over the two new kitchen doors that had been made in pine, but were meant to look like oak. Instant success – I discovered that if you put the paint on thinly enough, the grain still showed.

I now keep a wood colour mixed specially for painting on to wood which I use as a good base colour and alter in small quantities depending on what I am painting.

There are many other textures to choose from: marbling (see page 62) is done with a feather and gives an elegant appearance; sponging (see page 61) has a mottled effect; ragging produces a crumpled-newspaper effect, while spattering looks like a sort of speckled-bird's egg. I have concentrated on the techniques that I like best which do not include the last two.

Pattern

Pattern may be a line of swags and bows, the decorations round the top of a dado or cornice, a repeated stencil design or a complete picture such as a freehand floral design, a trompe l'oeil of your own devising or an ancient design taken from a book.

Another source of inspiration has been the crewel work of the seventeenth century. Insects, butterflies and snails were introduced into the embroideries, mainly as space fillers. I find that, rather than fillers, I use them as an integral part of the design where they can add life and wit. The butterflies are always playing 'catch me if you can' with rather exotic birds. I find myself caught up in their imaginary world, as the butterfly speeds past with long legs, just being missed by the ever watchful bird.

I first started using birds when I moved to London as they reminded me of the countryside. Each bird has his or her own personality which seems to evolve over the years and I feel I know my birds quite well by now.

Speckled, marbled or sponged backgrounds can be created on tiles as well as direct on to walls. These are popular at the moment and go well with the speckled, sponged or marbled china which is also fashionable.

(Opposite) 'Black and white cat washing itself with a butterfly hovering near by', 1987. The background foliage is flame-of-the-forest tree flowers.

This cherub or putto is a detail from my bedroom ceiling. Unlike the ones normally seen in churches, my cherubs have rosy, smiling faces – I always found them so bad-tempered-looking and spiteful as they hover over long-dead corpses!

Part two:

My Paint Techniques

CHAPTER THREE

Walls

Walls have been painted since time immemorial. The ancient Egyptians were the first to develop the mural into a high art form, although only using two dimensions. Wall painting spread to Babylon and Assyria; the Greeks and Romans used the effect to create an illusion of space and extra architectural embellishment when painting their villa walls. However, it was not until the fourteenth century that the Florentine painters developed the true three-dimensional mural as we know it today. This enabled the painter to 'deceive the eye' – *trompe l'oeil* as it is technically known. Perhaps the greatest contemporary muralist was Rex Whistler, whose marvellous, detailed landscapes again raised the mural to the status of a true work of art.

This was one of my more stupid ideas, as I was to discover to my cost when I suggested rather glibly that it would look wonderful to paint the whole exterior of the house with a stone finish. The client leapt at the idea and I was soon to find myself up a twenty-two-foot ladder balancing paint pots, sponges and brushes clenched between my teeth. Several months later, whilst a surveyor was inspecting the property he remarked on the unusual quality of the stone – this did not fill one with confidence as to his expertise!

Preparing the Surfaces

Walls should be dry, smooth and hard before decorating. Clean them down with a mild solution of sugar soap and water, using a clean car sponge. Fill any holes or cracks and rub back any broken surfaces with sandpaper.

If working on battered French, it won't matter if the wall is smoothly uneven or even slightly cracked. This will all add realism to the ultimate finish.

How to Measure Up Wall Areas for Panelling

Decide on the size of the panels you want and how high you want them to reach: either picture-rail height or dado height. Measure the whole room, transferring the dimensions to a room plan drawn up on paper. The plan and measurements need to be exact, as the finished effect will be more realistic if care is taken from the start. Begin with the longest wall. Calculate how many complete panels will fit into the length, allowing for an upright (stile) between each panel. Uprights are usually 4in (10cm) wide. If you have space to spare, either adjust the size of the panels to take up the extra, or, even better, adjust the width of the uprights. If the space is just a little tight, you can make a corner upright slimmer or double the width of the others. Final measurements can only be determined when you have assessed the whole room.

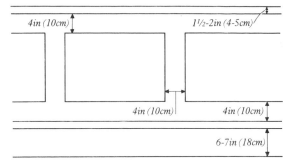

The sketch shows how the calculations might work out, starting with a basic panel width of 24in (60cm). As you can see, on the two longest walls I widened the panels slightly to fill the wall, while on the window wall there was enough room for a half-panel. Two panels fitted almost exactly along the door wall by just shaving 1in (2.5cm) off one of the uprights. Behind the door is a small filler panel with just one upright.

The division of the panel measurements can be determined according to the size of the room and the sort of effect you wish to create. I tend to use the same measurements throughout the house so that some sort of continuity is kept, creating an air of space and letting the eye travel evenly from one room area to another.

Treatment of Radiators, Doors and Skirtings

There's not much to say about radiators except that they are hell to decorate. I spend hours trying to blend them in with the rest of

(Left) This diagram shows the usual measurements that I use when painting panelled dados.

As radiators are never things of beauty I always try to assimilate them into the wall design to make them disappear as much as possible. Unfortunately, I have now found that it is the first thing everybody notices, so that they become the talking point of the room! (Opposite, clockwise starting at the top right-hand), My stone fantasy finish bathroom radiator; Wood fantasy graining; The Tree of Life showing a ploughed field with grassy hillocks; The wooden grille work was dappled with grey and white marbling, and the wood surround was treated in a similar manner to the rest of the dado; Extravagant blue and white marbling in my brother's bathroom; Lilies in a tropical jungle radiator.

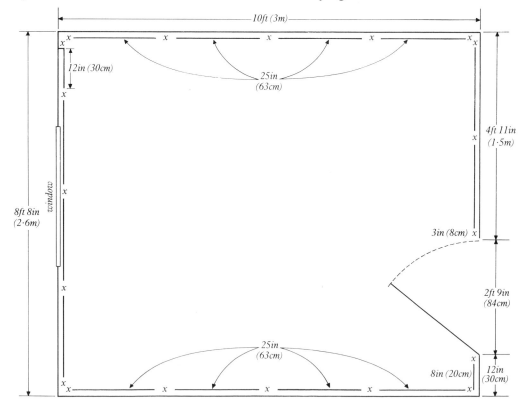

The diagram on the left gives simple directions for measuring up wall areas for panelling, which can be adapted to suit any room.

(Opposite, clockwise starting at top left-hand) I created this rather extravagant doorway to give grandeur to a tiny room, which acted as a frame to the 'Lady in Blue' portrait which is shown through the door on the back cover; grey and white marbled door carries on the feel of the dado and built-in sideboard (see page 62, bottom); I used the malachite recipe for this door, using different colourways to produce a delicate, faded stone effect. The walls are battered French with a marbled dado; the Tree of Life design was carried over the panelled door with some difficulty because of fitting the stencils over the panels; a different door using the malachite method and surrounded by stone finish walls in a shade of pale sandstone-terracotta; one of the few dragged doors. I used this simple finish because the door is right in the centre of the wall and I did not want the eye to be interrupted too much by making a feature of it.

the design and then often find that they are much admired! I usually try to hide doors and skirtings by covering them in the same paint finish as the rest of the room. I use emulsion and powder paints, just as I would for the walls.

Doors can have special features added in the panels, although the main part of the door should be kept in the same style as the windows and skirtings. Of course, there will always be the odd exception to every rule, like my little workroom (opposite, top left) where I decided to make a special design over the door. The door itself is quite plain but echoes the marbling used in the dado. Even though the room is small, I felt that the doorway should be imposing to complement the rest of the decoration in the room.

These are only two examples of many varied door treatments which are illustrated. I would say that the doorway is usually the last thing I work on in a room, since it is easier to decide what treatment to give it once the rest of the room is complete.

Antiquing Effects

These techniques are used after you have finished putting a special finish on a wall to add a sense of age and decay. There are two different ways of producing an instant antiqued or distressed look to a paint finish.

1. My 'Dirty Dishwater' Technique

This is my favourite method. Mix up a watery solution of black and red paint (the more red, the browner the end colour) which should resemble dirty dishwater. Apply a little of this to a clean damp car sponge with a brush. Quickly work across the entire sur-

face with an even action, leaving no lines or too obvious dragging marks. If some marks do occur, you can cautiously work over the area again, but don't rub too hard or a light area will appear, which could spoil the effect. If it is a little patchy, this will add to the worn appearance. The most important thing about this finish is that once you have started you cannot stop until the wall surface is covered, otherwise you will have a line which can never be concealed.

2. Sandpaper Technique

Allow the finished surface to dry completely (overnight or for twenty-four hours). Rub gently over the surface with fine sandpaper to lift off as much paint as you want. Don't overwork walls which have lining paper on them, or the joins will become lighter in tone than the rest of the wall.

Sponging

Sponging is a very useful technique and can be used in conjunction with other paint methods such as marbling. It gives a random, mottled finish which can look quite different depending on the sort of sponge used and how you apply it. There are many ways of sponging and mine is probably not very different from anyone else's!

Materials Needed

* A natural sponge about 4in (10cm) wide (the size of a large fist) which will comfortably fit into your cupped hand
* A bowl for mixing the paint
* An old plate
* Paint: base colour; sponging colour

(Right) Detail of Egyptian Lotus flowers design showing the sandpaper antiquing method described above. (Far right) This is one of the few examples of sponging on its own. The very fine effect was produced using a synthetic car sponge. The still life gives interest and depth to the alcove.

61

Method

Choose your sponge carefully for the size of its holes will determine the pattern on the wall. I prefer to use the top of the sponge, which gives a more delicate effect. The part which was attached to the seabed is often rather rough.

Apply the base colour to the walls and allow to dry. Water down the paint to the consistency of cream. Pour a little onto an old plate and gently dip the damp sponge onto the surface, just picking up enough paint to cover the top of the sponge.

Apply the paint to the wall, working at random so that you don't get a repeat pattern. If you overload the sponge, bash it out on an old newspaper to get rid of excess paint. If you make a mistake, paint over with the base colour and, when dry, fill in with more sponging. At the corners or in awkward places, use a small piece of old sponge or a brush and stipple lightly with the bristle ends to simulate the markings of the sponge.

Alternatively, soak the sponge in the paint, wring it out, then apply as above.

Dry Sponging

This is basically the same technique. The only difference is that the paint is mixed slightly thicker and is applied onto the dry natural sponge by carefully passing a loaded paint brush over the top, so that only the tips of the sponge are wet with paint. The effect is light and delicate.

Marbling

I specialize in fantasy marbling, marbling that can be used where the real thing could not be used – on cornices, skirting boards and window and door frames. This is based on a knowledge of how the veins would run on a real piece of marble. Marble is derived from fairly pure limestone, re-crystallized. It is usually given the name of the place where it is quarried or a name which describes its coloration. The most famous is Carrara marble from Italy, although marble is found throughout the world in many varied colours, depending on which type of co-existing rocks lie near the marble beds.

Marble is used extensively throughout the building trade, either polished or left in its raw state. Most marble dealers will be pleased to show you their stock of off-cut pieces which are often kept at the back of their premises. Study all the different colours and formations. Buying and becoming familiar with the occasional piece is a good

(Left) This was my brother's original marble fireplace, which unfortunately had had the top marble facing replaced with cement. At Henry's request, I marbled the cement to match the uprights.

(Left) My brother's bathroom. This was done as a birthday present. The instructions were to do a totally outrageous and over-the-top marbled effect in rather bright colours. The radiator (p. 59) was left until a year later as my brother somewhat pompously informed me that having central heating was a status symbol!

(Left) Two different aspects of a dining room marbled for an unseen client. I was relegated to deal through the estate agent and only met the clients long after the job was done. Fortunately, they loved it.

way to see how it is formed. You will note that in the veined type, the veins do not just wander around the place indiscriminately; they all have somewhere to go. There are never veins just stuck in midstream; they all join up at some point, mostly flowing like a river in the same direction, giving a random but structured design. (As a point of interest: in case you prefer the real thing to the painted effect, when transporting marble it is imperative to keep your slab upright. Do not lie it flat or it will crack and break in half.)

I have included two simple descriptions of marbling techniques.

Grey and White Marbling

Materials Needed

* Good quality 3in–4in (7.5cm–10cm) wide paint brush
* Chinese calligraphy brush with 2in (5cm) long bristle or sable pencil brush no. 4
* Softener brush 3in (7.5cm) wide, preferably badger
* Natural sponge, about 4in (10cm) diameter (the size of a large fist)
* Paint: base coat (cream emulsion); grey

Method

If you cannot obtain a good commercial grey colour, mix your own shade by buying powder or gouache in any of the following combinations: base white and black mixed with yellow ochre (for yellow-grey marble) or crimson lake (for pinkish-grey marble) or ultramarine (for blue-grey marble).

Paint the wall with two coats of cream emulsion and leave it to dry while you dilute the white base coat.

For the base coat, dilute the white paint to the consistency of water and paint across the entire surface, leaving the cream to show through in patches. Then work the clean sponge diagonally across the area to open it up and produce a clouded or mottled effect, lifting the paint off with the sponge.

Now blend your marbling colour in a mixing bowl, to form the grey of your choice. Add enough water to form a smooth paste. Then add white emulsion until the colour is the correct shade. Dilute a quantity of the grey paint to the consistency of thin cream and while the white surface is still wet, apply grey streaks with a brush, diagonally overlapping the white paint in places. These streaks should be 6in–10in (15cm–25cm) apart, depending on the size of the marble effect you want. Squeeze out the still whitened sponge and press over the entire surface to blend the colours and lift off excess

GREY AND WHITE MARBLING

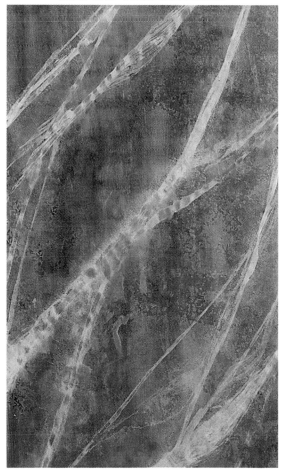

BLACK AND WHITE MARBLING

63

paint. Then, using a light vigorous fanning action, work over the surface, creating a soft clouded or faded effect.

While the surface is still damp, create the veins by applying the remaining grey paint with the Chinese or pencil brush, using bold strokes which follow the grey streaks. Let the brush 'jump' or 'stagger', twisting the hairs to make the lines vary from thick to thin. After some practice you will be able to achieve a realistic marble effect. The grey veins should all link up to each other and flow in the same direction with the occasional diagonal cross-over to the neighbouring strands. The effect is rather like a river with its tributaries. If you wish, you can firmly pat the larger veins at random leaving untouched sections, which will lift out the middle area of the vein, leaving a very thin line either side with only a faint suggestion of colour in the middle.

Blend the veining immediately with the badger softener brush, using a light but vigorous fanning action from side to side and then up and down to draw out the streaks and fade the lines.

Black Marbling

Materials Needed:
* At least one feather
* Thin pencil brush
* Squirrel fan brush
* Two pudding basins or largish bowls
* Bowl of water
* Natural sponge
* Large plate
* Paint: base colour (black); second colour (pale grey); third colour (white)

Method

Prepare the surface by sanding, filling and generally cleaning it. Mix up a pale grey paint colour in one bowl and white in another to a consistency of thin cream and pour a little of each onto the plate. Apply two coats of black emulsion paint to the surface to be decorated. When the second coat is still damp, start doing the veining with a feather or brush. The dampness enables the paint to mix in with the base coat producing variations in colour.

Pass the feather over the paint, wiping any overload off on the side of the plate while twisting the feather spines into lines. With a firm, steady movement, paint in the veins. You may use the feather in two different ways, either uncut, or, to produce more exotic veining, with some of the spines cut out with a scalpel to give the feather a toothy

appearance (see diagram). Practise a little on some rough paper or a wall as yet untreated.

When you have finished with the light grey, you need to remove some of the paint. Press the fresh paint with a damp sponge, trying to use a clean area of the sponge with every dab, to soften the veining, or wait until the veining is nearly dry and dab so that the middle of the vein comes off leaving the two outer edges.

Another method is to use a squirrel fan brush and, with an extremely light fanning movement from side to side, dust over the top of the veining to pull the paint in very fine lines sideways, opening up the veins. (If you are marbling over an ogee moulding, proceed as above, touching in the concave parts of the moulding afterwards with a brush.) Then with the white paint, introduce a few white lines to one side of the line of grey so high-lighting the grey. Dab or fan off as before.

Battered French

I once spent some weeks in Italy and arrived in Verona late at night and out of petrol. I stayed the night in a small pensione in the main square, and went to bed exhausted after eating deliciously and joining in the fête that was being held in the town. Next morning I woke up to discover that wonderful, crumbling city with its beautiful peeling terracotta colours and its yellow-ochre painted house fronts.

For many years I tried to imitate this state of disrepair, and it was only much later that I really started to master the technique. Even now I am finding new ways of doing it every

MARBLING FEATHERS

(Left) The stencil design over the doorway echoes the dado panels set against battered French walls. (Opposite) The most simple table can be dressed with cloth, brocades and, in this case, an antique sleeping blanket from Tunisia. (Overleaf) I painted the walls of this drawing room in battered French but had to add a dado as the room was so high that the battered French paint dried too quickly to maintain a constant effect.

64

time I take up my brush. The idea is to achieve that decayed elegance where everything appears sumptuous but faded. The English have their version of this; like an over-blown rose, soft and easy to live with (where a few cat hairs won't matter).

Materials Needed

* ★ Car sponge
* ★ Small paint brush
* ★ Paint: base colour of dull pink (although you can choose any colour you like); antiquing colour of sludge grey

Method

Paint the areas to be covered with one or two coats of base colour, as required. If the wall is slightly uneven, so much the better for the ultimate finish. Mix the antiquing colour while waiting for the base coat to dry. Use an antiquing colour of sludge grey or dusty brown and make it very watery.

Soak and squeeze the sponge in water, then apply the thinned paint to it with a brush and start application on the smallest wall area of the room to give yourself some practice. Turn the heating down low and work in a cool atmosphere if possible, so that the paint won't dry out too quickly. If this occurs, add a teaspoon of glycerine to your watery paint, which slows down the drying process.

I normally work from the ceiling down. Use sweeping movements, smoothing out the sponge marks, so that the whole effect is naturally aged, without lines or sponge marks. Don't stop until you have finished the whole wall or there will be a line right up the wall which you won't be able to get rid of. And don't overwork any one area or you will be left with a lighter patch. If you find one appearing, just leave it. At the corners, use a mop brush loaded with thinned paint and quickly work down the corner, sponging the paint smooth with your other hand as you go along.

Have a good rest between walls and remember that you will need a lot of practice for this technique. The thinner the wash, the more difficult it is to apply, as the plaster or paper sucks out the pigment, leaving just water to be sponged about. Speed is of the essence.

Since I started incorporating dados into my room designs, I have discovered that with 3 feet (1 metre) taken away from the wall height, this method has become far more successful because the wall area is more manageable.

Stone Finishes

I find stone among the more pleasing finishes. It seems to give a clean and restful, yet aged, finish. Stone projects the image of grandeur and lends a certain classicism to a house. I used a stone finish in my bathroom to give the idea of looking over a stone-walled balcony with terracotta urns set against a blue sky (see page 69). Sometimes, as I sit in the bath, I feel the effect is so realistic that it is hard to imagine that I actually did it. I begin to analyze how it was achieved, and what mix of colours were used, before I freeze to death and have to get out to warm up under a huge towel.

Materials Needed

* ★ Charcoal
* ★ Fitch
* ★ Bowl of water
* ★ Car sponge or natural sponge
* ★ Damp rag
* ★ Paint: three different colours (white or cream emulsion, grey base paint and grey with a little black added).

On one of my visits to Milan I was wined and dined in an amazing restaurant with bare light bulbs and scrubbed tables with soft, worn, plaster walls; the kitchen here is a direct result of those memories.

The stone dado gives the illusion of a Roman balcony with urns giving on to distant vistas of the hills on a sultry day whilst you lie cooling off in your bath. This effect was deliberately created to counteract the lack of windows in an internal bathroom. (See also page 91.)

Method

Having prepared your surface in the usual manner, apply two coats of white or cream emulsion. While this is drying off, you can decide what sort of stone finish you want to paint. The variety of stone coloration is enormous: sandstone being really quite yellow, for example, whereas granite is more grey-black in tone.

Mix up enough paint so that it can be divided into several amounts, depending on how many colours you want to use; then you can add different colours to lighten or darken the main base colour. Apply the base grey haphazardly over the area with a damp car sponge, leaving some areas untouched. Start applying the second colour (your base colour with some black added) before the first is dry. Carry on as before, but sponge less and leave the cream or white along with the paler grey to show through in larger patches. If the colour seems to be getting too dark, mix some white into the base grey. You can add some warmth to the general effect by mixing up a deep creamy yellow ochre and dropping in a small quantity of black to deaden the

sharpness of the yellow. Be careful not to end up with green. Apply either or both colours with a damp sponge to give a natural dappled effect. The more shades you add, overlapping one colour on another, the more depth the 'stone' will have. The whole thing may now appear to be a blotchy mess, but the next process will pull it all together.

Water down the grey paint to a very thin 'dishwater' colour. The thinner you can manage, the better. You can always apply another coat if the effect is not right. Use the car sponge to wipe over the entire surface to blend all the colours, leaving the different applications of paint looking like faded undertone with the slightly grainy texture of natural stone.

After applying several different coats of water-based paint, the whole area will now have to be measured accurately and marked out. Allow the paint to dry out completely. There are two methods for marking out the stone squares. The first is to draw up your squares in either charcoal or chalk. Using a damp rag wrapped round your index finger, rub over your marked lines without pressing too hard (or the white will show through) to leave you with a soft suggestion of lining. As this takes hours to accomplish, I would suggest that you employ the second method.

Using the thinned grey paint, with a length of picture rail as a rule, apply the cement fillets with a fitch. The charcoal will add shading to the lines. If you have used the stone effect for a dado only, you can finish off the top rail with a 2in (5cm) line all round the room in the same colour as the lining, adding a lighter grey line to simulate light falling onto the top of the stone wall.

Incidentally, if you decide to include a keystone over a doorway, as shown immediately below, you should remember that the blocks of 'stone' must be drawn from the base up, as they would have been built using real stone.

(Above) Country house hallway showing a vista of the stone finish. (Above, left) Detail of stepped 'stonework' over a doorway. (Left) Exterior of the same house (pages 56–7) at dusk, painted by me in a granite stone finish.

Wood Painted to Look Like Wood

Wood graining by painting is a long and tedious operation. This method is a quick and easy way to make wood the colour you want it to be. It works on furniture and panelling and I have used it on figured (i.e. grained) blockboard too. In my bathroom, blockboard was used for the ends and splash-back (made removeable in the event of a blocked pipe).

The blockboard was sanded, filled and undercoated with flat oil-based paint to prevent water penetration, then given the dark brown wood treatment. Even I am impressed, and others will not believe it is only blockboard not oak that they are busy admiring. This is a cheap and simple solution to a nicely fitted bath.

I have also used this technique on a plate rack and on the wooden part of the fireplace with the cement slips (see below). The fireplace surround is made of oak, which got splattered with paint. Rather than remove the paint, I decided to paint the wood to look like wood!

Materials Needed

* Sandpaper
* Wood filler
* Brushes
* Oil-based undercoat for wet areas, if needed
* Paint (mixed to look like the wood you are simulating)
* Button polish or matt polyurethane
* Car sponge

(Above) The tiny bathroom shown here illustrates how one can paint blockboard to look like seasoned oak. (Right) The plate rack above two panelled doors all painted in the same method. (Far right) The oak fireplace which I didn't have time to strip so instead painted to look like oak.

Method

This is the method that I have developed for bath panels or when using unfigured blockboard.

On blockboard, if there is no grain, you can apply a white undercoat. When this is dry, drag the thinned brown paint over the surface. This should achieve a straight, grained effect. Depending on what wood you are simulating, mix your paints to a red-brown for mahogany or a blackish-brown for old oak. Either seal with matt polyurethane or button polish.

I cannot live without a plate rack, so every time I move, some poor person has the job of drilling hundreds of holes to fit the pieces of dowelling together. I have found that it is more successful to paint ramin (a special hard wood used for dowelling) as it takes up the dye in a patchy manner.

Mixing a watery consistency of brown paint to the colour you want. Apply with a brush or car sponge and leave to dry. This same method has been used for the two panelled kitchen doors (page 71) with great success.

Once I made up this method, I found myself rushing round the house, brush in hand, operating miracles all over the place.

Fantasy Wood Graining

Visiting Ham House for about the fifth time, I thought the wood graining could be adapted for my hallway and stairs. This house is so crammed full of everything from the sixteenth and seventeenth centuries that it is impossible to take in all the information at one visit, so I now go back to restudy it every time I have a new bee in my bonnet.

Materials Needed

* Chalk or charcoal
* Car sponge
* Pipe-over brush
* 1in (2.5cm) fitch
* 2in (5cm) long-haired Chinese calligraphy brush or pencil brush no. 4
* Length of picture framing
* Black and white emulsion
* Crimson lake powder
* Softener

Method

The base coat was applied with the panels measured and marked out with chalk in the same manner as the panelled bedroom on page 58. It helps to look at some examples of

wood before you start. I was lucky as the carpets were not laid, so I was able to copy the well-worn floorboards as I proceeded along the hallway and up the stairs.

Having let your base brown dry thoroughly, mix up an almost black emulsion to a single cream consistency. Apply the colour with either a Chinese calligraphy brush or a no. 4 pencil brush. Start in the middle of the panel (the heart of the tree, so to speak), and mark outwards – painting the rings so that some are close together whilst others are 2 to 3 inches apart. These lines delineate the growth which the tree has made in a year and if there was a drought this is indicated by the increased closeness of one line to the next. Before the paint dries use a clean, dry brush to fan the lines as in marble veining, only this time go straight up and down *not* side to side. Pull the top of your arch out as much as you can.

When you have finished all the graining, paint the uprights in simple veins from top to bottom using the dark paint and a pipe-over brush. This is repeated on the parallels at the top and bottom of the panels as well as the skirting board. The grain in this case goes from side to side. Then mix some white into your graining paint and line each panel on the bottom and one side (see page 19). The top and opposite side are in shadow therefore paint these with the dark mix.

Then apply a light line to the top edge of the dado and you can also use the antiquing methods described on page 61, if that is the effect you want to create.

The radiator shows the best example of the fantasy wood graining described on this page, offset by a Georgian hand-carved and gilded vine-leaf pattern mirror. This is one of my favourite photographs, as I love the reflection of the painting of the rich red robes of the painting of the cardinal.

| 'oak' with marked perimeter | stencil in pale blue | light shading on stencil | dark shading on stencil | gold highlighting | finished stencil, antiqued |

original stencil

The six stages to achieving the Elizabethan panelled bedroom stencils. The last illustration shows the actual stencil well used and (overleaf) the final effect in my bedroom.

Stencils and the Way I Use Them

Generally speaking, I do not particularly like stencil designs and use them only if I want to repeat a design or part of a design several times (see pages 74–5). Of course, stencils make the work much quicker (and so cheaper for clients), since there is no need to paint every leaf on a tree by hand. I over-painted the stencil by adding leaf veining or light and shade. The important thing from my point of view is that the end result should not look printed. I try to make the designs look as unstencilled as possible, taking risks by not cutting as many legs or bridges (joining pieces) which are important in holding the stencil together, if they are not an integral part of the design. The Japanese, who are the masters of stencil cutting, use human hair to stop their designs from falling apart. As yet I have not tried this.

I do not use a stencil brush, although I do own one or two. I find using them leaves me with aching arms so now I use a quicker method, which is a sponge. Nor do I protect the surrounding area with paper or bother with masking tape unless the stencil is too large to hold. As for hingeing my stencils to facilitate going round corners (this is when you cut the stencil paper at the point where it meets the corner, then rejoin with masking tape on both sides) – I just bend them, which seems to suffice. I imagine this is what's called being lazy but I get the effect that satisfies me.

Materials Needed

* Stencil paper (cartridge paper soaked in linseed oil). If this is not large enough, join two sheets together, putting masking tape on both sides
* Charcoal or chalk
* Black felt tip pen
* Scalpel or matte knife
* Fitch, ½in (1.5cm) or 1in (2.5cm)
* Small natural sponge (a face sponge is ideal) and clean car sponge
* Masking tape
* White emulsion, black emulsion, crimson lake powder, ultramarine powder, gold paint or powders

Method (for stencilling onto panels)

Measure the dimensions of the room carefully, then draw the room plan on paper as described on page 58. When you know how large each panel will be, draw your design in chalk or charcoal onto the stencil paper. Many people use acetate for stencils, but I find it slippery and hard to cut, so I nearly always use stencil paper. Outline your design in felt pen so as not to smudge the lines when cutting. If necessary shade the areas to be cut out. Start in the middle of the stencil. Press hard enough with the knife to cut clean edges the first time, otherwise you will have to go round the stencil cleaning up, which is boring and time-consuming.

If the design is large, be careful not to bend or break any thinly cut parts. If this should

occur, repair the damage immediately with masking tape on both sides, then cut out the shape again.

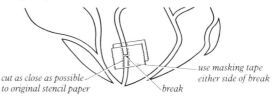

cut as close as possible to original stencil paper

use masking tape either side of break

break

MENDING A STENCIL

If you have to repeat the stencil many times, it may be a wise precaution to stencil the design onto another piece of stencil paper, in case the first one gets damaged beyond repair or clogged up with paint. Don't bother to cut it out until you need it. Now you are ready to go.

Prepare the walls as usual with white emulsion paint and leave to dry. Draw a line round the room at the height you want the panelling to finish, using a yardstick. Mix up the colours you want for the base coat of the panelling (in this case a warm brown, adding crimson lake to black emulsion until the colour resembles seasoned oak. Thin the paint to the consistency of milk, and apply with a sponge as in battered French (see page 64). Don't worry if the finish is not particularly smooth, but take care not to leave visible sponge marks. Gently rub over the uneven areas with the sponge, creating lighter patches to indicate the change in natural wood.

Leave the paint to dry, then mark with chalk where the uprights should go between each panel, to indicate exactly where the stencil should be placed.

Mix ultramarine and black emulsion powder to a paste then add to the white emulsion to form a blue-grey or duck-egg colour. It should be the consistency of thick cream. Pour a small amount onto a plate, spreading it out with a brush.

Because this is a big stencil, place the stencil paper in position with masking tape at top, waist and bottom. Don't press the tape too hard or you may lift off the base colour when you remove it. Dip the face sponge onto the plate, being careful not to overload the sponge. Dab the stencil quickly and lightly all over, trying to avoid any paint running under the stencil, although this can be corrected during the shading stage. Remove the completed stencil, touching up the 'leg' marks immediately, and repeat this process until the room is finished.

Close-up of the Elizabethan four-poster bed, showing the fabulously arcaded headboard inlaid with geometric designs in bog oak, holly and boxwood.

75

Divide the remaining blue paint in half. To one half, add black to make a darker blue-grey and, to the other half, white to make a softer, lighter colour.

Look carefully at the overall light pattern in the room and decide whether the light is coming in from the left or the right.

Shade your stencil accordingly. Use the fitch to run down the outside edge of the panel with the aid of a picture frame or ruler, painting the side in shadow with the darker blue, then repeating the process on the other side of the panel, where the light is falling, with the paler blue.

Now shade the leaves and berries in the same way, repeating the technique used for the borders of the panels.

I have used gold powders (see page 83) as an extra highlight on the berries and the sides of each panel.

If you wish to antique the stencilled panelling, use either method described on page 61.

Painting on to Glazed Wall Tiles

Normally I use tiles made in whichever country I'm in; you are assured of being able to buy any quantity whenever you like and they have a shorter shelf life, which is important, as the longer a tile is stored the more it absorbs moisture, making it more liable to break when re-fired. Try to avoid chipped or cracked tiles, otherwise you run the risk of them splitting and breaking the other tiles.

I find that glazed tiles are much nicer to work on as the onglaze (the glaze used on a commercially glazed tile) can be wiped off if you make a mistake, whereas with unglazed tiles you cannot wash the underglaze off and these tiles therefore need firing twice.

The onglaze colours are true to life, except for red, which needs handling with care as it can go brown if accidentally mixed with other colours. Even though mixed, this medium doesn't 'go off' so can be used months later. This is just as well, since a small tube of onglaze is too expensive to waste. Once mixed, all leftovers can be kept in their dishes for further use. Remember to blow the dust off first! If you do suffer the odd breakage, it is not too difficult to replace, especially if you do not wash-up your mixtures until all the tiles are successfully fired.

A small kiln made by Harrison Meyer, which holds up to seventeen tiles, is not too expensive to buy. If it is only a one-off job, you can rent kiln space from a potter.

To paint a picture on tiles, I use the dining room table protected with a cloth, I spread out the tiles, pushing them close together.

76

(Left, above) Pears in a blue and white bowl on antiqued tiles. (Left, below) Gilded vase with Persian roses standing on a blue and white Topkapi plate with yellow pears, also antiqued. (Below) The pink peacock, surrounded by tiny butterflies, looking down at a snail.

Draw the outline of your design with a fine pencil brush in black onglaze, cleaning any mistakes with lavatory paper or cotton wool buds. Wash off the whole design if you don't like it under the tap. Make sure the tile is properly dry before repainting. For inspiration have a look in the back of this book which gives you an idea of a few effects you could achieve.

When the tiles are ready to put in the racks, pick them up, being very careful not to touch the glaze, otherwise it will come off. For technical firing instructions, follow the methods recommended in the booklet which comes with your kiln.

Antiquing Tiles
Materials Needed

* Dirty dishwater colour
* Natural sponge
* Badger hair fan brush or 2in (5cm) Hamilton's paint brush

Method

As I have explained, the onglaze is extremely delicate so care is needed. When your design is dry, you can practise one of two methods.

Mix up a very watery, dirty-dishwater colour using the onglaze colours predominant in the design, e.g. leftovers. Squeeze out a natural sponge in the mix and then gently apply, just as you would to walls, all over the design. You will see that the colours lift and become slightly blurred and mottled.

The alternate method is to use a badger hair fan brush or 2in (5cm) Hamilton's paint brush. You need to practise or else you could end up with very little glaze left on the tiles. Really gently, fan the brush over the surface to literally 'wear off' the glaze as much as you want. Blow off the glaze dust and particles so that they will not become part of the design when fired. The method leaves the tiles looking softly worn.

(Opposite) Magnolia tree with Birds-of-Paradise. (Below, left) Big Poo and Baby Poo. (Below, right) The ginger cat staring at the Burmese. (Bottom) A chocolate-point who was called Feng Tai.

Creating a Speckled, Marbled or Sponged Background

Materials Needed

* ★ Natural sponge
* ★ Pencil brush

Method

Basically you can use the same methods as you would when painting walls. (See Sponging and Marbling on pages 61 and 62.) Bear in mind that if this method is to be used as background cover only, you will need to fire the tiles before doing a design on the top, which runs the risk of breaking, although I have had no trouble and find it worth the effort.

Once the tiles have been fired they are extremely durable, as the onglaze melts at a temperature of approximately 780°–820° centigrade into the base glaze, fusing the glazes. I mostly clean mine with the aid of a scouring pad when they get really dirty.

79

Furniture

Furniture can be completely changed with the addition of a painted finish. So long as the piece has a good shape with elegant lines it can be put back 'in period' or treated in a modern manner. This is not only achieved with techniques of dragging, sponging or semi-precious stone finishes: colour also plays a very important part. Colours can be subtle or bright, antiqued or simply left as natural. Swags of flowers, leaves or fruit can be added to enhance your paint effect. Refurbishing furniture also includes re-upholstery, which can be done with second-hand or redyed cotton velvets and hand-painted calico to which are added gimps or tassels.

This bed was made of fruitwood which suffers dramatically from warping and worm, so the only solution was to paint it. I actually used the split and warped panels which had the advantage of ageing the bed in a realistic manner. The side of the bed was painted with tulips and other flowers often used in seventeenth- and eighteenth-century oil paintings. The curling tendrils of the trailing columbines fused the overall design. This was then somewhat brutally antiqued to complement the twisted wood and wormholes.

RESTORATION OF PAINTED FURNITURE

I would not recommend that you restore any furniture of value, unless you have made an in-depth study of the correct techniques. What follows are useful hints to help you touch up recently painted pieces.

My ideal is to touch up only where really necessary, where there are repairs or totally rotten areas, leaving most of the original painted finish behind, so that the table, or whatever, is left in its original state as far as possible.

The way to tell the correct shade of colour is to remember that when the paint is wet, it is the colour it will be when sealed or polished. If the paint is to be left totally untreated, which is very rare, you must make tests on paper and wait for the paint to dry. A useful tip is that when the polish is dulled, you can find out its true colour by rubbing a little spit over a small area.

Most of the furniture I buy for re-painting is Victorian or later reproductions of earlier times. This is usually solid and well-made, and the main thing is that you are not ruining a precious antique.

Preparation of Surfaces

Before painting a piece of furniture, it should be in a state of good repair. If there are any chipped mouldings or loose legs, fill or re-glue. Then, having made sure that your wood is dry, clean off any dust or dirt. If the piece is polished, wipe over with a rag soaked in methylated spirits. Leave to dry. Sand to obtain a 'key' for your paint. Prime and undercoat if you wish.

Gilding

Gilding is a very similar method to the application of metal leaf, but requires ten times more groundwork.

At first I thought it was necessary to explain the techniques of this procedure, but on reflection, I have decided that you really can survive with the metal leaf process, since it is not only cheaper but less harassing. The preparation of the base is no different from any other piece of furniture and there are no long hours of applying gesso.

My attitude is that when and if you wish to learn how to gild, do it properly by going on a specialized course.

Metal Finishes

Dutch Metal Leaf

Dutch metal leaf is certainly the next best. This is what I call 'poor man's gold'. It is a cheap method of simulating gold leaf, but far easier to apply as it is much stronger.

Metal leaf is bought in book form just like gold leaf. It is made up of metal beaten very thinly and mounted on sheets of waxed paper. There are two colours, gold and silver (which is aluminium). The aluminium can be made to simulate gold by applying orange-coloured button polish (though this is hardly worth the trouble as it is not much cheaper than gold), or aged silver by washing over the surface with diluted Indian inks or umber, which will suggest a tarnished look.

Materials Needed

* ★ Gold size
* ★ Gold or aluminium metal leaf
* ★ Cotton wool or fairly stiff brush
* ★ Button polish
* ★ Soft brush
* ★ Lint-free rag
* ★ Indian ink (diluted with water)

Method

Make sure the gold size is of good quality, and then colour it slightly so that you can see where you have applied it. Follow the instructions on the tin. Apply it to the area and then leave it until touch dry (slightly tacky). It is quite important that the size should be at the right stage, as this does affect the lustre of the leaf which is dulled if applied on to a wet ground. Do a little test with a piece of metal leaf. The leaf is applied to the size gold-side down. If it sticks properly without sliding you are ready to start.

Some people work with a pad of cotton wool but I prefer to work with a fairly stiff brush. The brush size will depend on the area of the surface but it should certainly be no bigger than 1in (2.5cm).

Firmly and evenly pounce (a stabbing movement) the brush over the paper. Make sure, when you are metalling carved pieces, that you work the leaf into the crevices as deeply as you can. Gently lift off the paper and proceed with the adjacent area, placing the leaf overlapping the part just completed, always from the same side, so that you will not see the leaf joins. When the whole area is covered, gently brush off any loose metal on the joins with a soft brush. If there are any missed areas (known professionally as 'skips' or 'holidays'), repair these by re-applying

This is an Empire bed in fruitwood. Unfortunately, it was in such bad repair that I decided the only way of restoring it to its former glory was to paint it black and then Dutch metal it. This, some might say, was a terrible crime but it wasn't the greatest antique that ever hit earth.

metal leaf over the defect and brushing off the surplus.

All metal leaf must be sealed with a couple of coats of button polish, or it tends to flake off.

For a silver finish, use aluminium leaf, applied in the same manner. When it has dried, seal the leaf with several coats of button polish.

Brush diluted Indian ink over the entire surface.

If you want to highlight it, wet a lint-free rag with methylated spirits and, before the paint has totally hardened, gently buff off any protruding areas.

Gold Powders

If used with imagination, gold powders can pass for bashed-up gold leaf. Gold powders are also a quick, cheap method and I keep a constant stock of two different colours of bronze powders: Rich super gold No. 140 and light-orange super gold No. 160.

Materials Needed

* Two colours of gold powder as above
* A bowl kept specially for this job which seldom needs to be cleaned
* Button or liquid polish
* Beeswax polish
* Fine brush
* Jam jar of methylated spirits
* White emulsion paint
* 'Dirty dishwater' coloured paint (optional)
* Fine sandpaper
* Stiff paper or newspaper

Method

Put half and half of each colour of the gold powder in two small piles side by side. Then pour a small pool of button polish into the bowl and mix in a small amount of gold powder at a time, since it dries out very quickly. I mix only the amount I need for the next few minutes. Taking random amounts of the two different golds into the polish so that there is an uneven colour, apply to the piece of furniture with a brush. There should be enough powder in the mix so that it actually comes out gold. Sometimes it can be a bit watery, in which case you just add more gold. On the other hand, if the mix should start drying out, add more button polish. Clean the brush immediately the job is completed or you will have to throw it away. Keep a jam jar of methylated spirits next to you to put the brush into because even stopping to answer the phone may give the brush time to dry out.

Antiquing Metalled Finishes

If you wish to antique the gold in a 'worn' way, first apply a base coat of white paint. Let this dry, then paint on the colour coat. When that is dry, brush on the gold powder mix. Work the gold well into the crevices if the area is carved. When it has dried, sand gently back to the white (which passes for gesso), exposing some wood on the high points where the paint would naturally wear off.

Alternatively, you could apply a coat of 'dirty dishwater' colour, which should be well brushed into the crevices to simulate dust or dirt. Before it is dry, lift off with a sponge to expose the protruding areas or, if the surface is flat, just make it blotchy.

Another method is to use the base-colour paint. This should only be put onto the protruding areas. Take a squidge of stiff paper, crush it into creases and then press the base-colour paint over the gold so that you have a peeling effect.

Leave both methods until well dry and seal with liquid or button polish. Polish to a shine or leave matt.

All the metal finishes described above can be further antiqued by using wire wool or sandpaper to expose the raw wood, in places where the piece of furniture receives most handling.

Malachite

Malachite was normally used as polished veneers for small table boxes, ornaments and decorative furniture. It was also crushed and used as an inorganic pigment known as mountain green.

It is the most exciting and exotic of semi-precious stones. Used in some quantity by the Russians, Catherine the Great was most partial to this wonderful creation which has properties totally different from any other stone when used for decorative purposes.

You must have guessed that I'm mad about it! Any excuse to use it and I do. It is usually found where there are copper deposits, hence the intense green. The best examples can be seen in St Isaac's Cathedral and the hall facings of the Winter Palace in Leningrad, should you find yourself in their vicinity.

If you are not visiting Russia, the next best place to see examples is in a natural history museum or perhaps large shops with a department selling semi-precious stones. I suggest that you try to have a look at the real thing to see what wonderful possibilities it has.

When I started reading other people's methods of achieving this stone simulation, it all seemed too complicated, so I started off experimenting to find a quicker method. The main one I use is in slab form.

Materials Needed

For American readers, read eraser for rubber.
* Squirrel fan brush no. 5
* Sandpaper and duster
* Liquid polish
* A 1½–2in (3.5–4cm) square rubber
* An oblong rubber with a flat end
* A typewriter correction rubber, or pencil rubber
* Rubber date stamp
* Scalpel
* Goose feathers or 2 squirrel mop brushes
* Damp cloth or old flannel
* Paint (viridian green powder; chrome yellow powder; black emulsion)
* Varnish or liquid polish

A Victorian classic four-panelled door can be given a heightened sense of grandeur by adding decoration to the panels. In this particular instance, I have adapted the acanthus leaf dado design to fit the narrow panels.

Method

Prepare the surface in the normal way by generally cleaning off any dirt and repairing badly damaged parts.

Mix up a true emerald-green paint colour. Emerald green is mixed using viridian green and chrome, added to black. The chrome brings out the emerald. This is painted onto the area with a squirrel mop. Leave to dry. A second coat will be needed. Next, brush on to the surface two coats of liquid polish. Allow to dry between each coat. While waiting for it to dry, mix up a very dark green: viridian added to black. This paint should be the consistency of single cream. Until you are experienced, you will have problems stopping the paint from drying out on a surface larger than 12in (30cm) square, although the thing about this method is that if you make a real bish the whole lot can be wiped off before it dries, and you can start again immediately.

Again, if you are half-way through your work and you notice a skin appearing, rub off that part and reapply the dark-green paint. The join will not really show when dry, dissolving into the background as another fault in the rock formation. However, I would suggest that you try the technique out on a piece of hardboard first, then you will not feel so nervous.

Line up your implements: a cut rubber (this is done with a scalpel, see illustration), a date stamp made of rubber, a goose feather and a damp cloth or old flannel. It it important to 'degunge' the equipment by wiping it onto the damp flannel after each stage. With another squirrel mop, spread the very dark green paint over the entire surface. Test to see if the paint is ready by pulling the rubber over the surface. If the paint is still too wet the line will close up again. Leave it for a few minutes, using the rubber test fairly frequently. When the rubber marks stand out clearly, the paint has reached the correct tackiness. You will have to work quickly from now on.

You will see from the illustration of the rubber that there are several different teeth and edges cut on all sides. These are aids to produce the variation of line width, and so is the rubber date stamp. Using part (a) of the rubber, work quickly from the centre wiping the surface in elliptical sweeps. Use the rubber on alternate (a), (b), (c) sides, making bold circular movements. Jerking and creating zig-zags and pleats, alternate this process with the rubber date stamp to create fine lines. Small circles, dots and dabs are made by pressing the flat end of an oblong rubber

Picture of a bunch of asparagus laid on a malachite slab. The client who bought this painting especially requested that the frame should also be done in malachite with black lacquer. This is not easy to do because of the mouldings either side of the 2in (5cm) flat bed of the frame. I would suggest that if you want to do a similar frame you malachite the plank before adding the mouldings.

on to the paint and simply twisting clockwise. Fine lines can be added around each circle by using a pencil rubber.

When you have completed this most alarming of experiences first time round, before the paint dries, use the larger side of the goose feather or squirrel fan brush and, ever so lightly, hardly touching the surface, pass across the lines, wriggling the feather very gently so that the veins are not straight but appear wavy. These tiny, tiny veins run across the grain. It also softens and almost marbles the surface.

Leave your creation to dry for at least twenty-four hours, then seal either with several coats of liquid polish or, if the piece is being subjected to heavy use, varnish. The more coats that are applied, the stronger the depth of the finish will be. I have read that as many as fifty coats should be painted onto all stone finishes, but that's up to you! Maintenance involves polishing occasionally, as for any other piece of furniture. Malachite finish is really worth trying and you will love it.

All the examples show slabs of malachite. You can, if you wish, divide the surface into irregular shapes to simulate veneers. I have tried it but feel that I can live without that effect. However, I will explain the principle so that you can try it too.

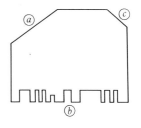

(Opposite) The German secretaire is shown here offset by a detail of the malachite finish. This clearly illustrates the effect created by using the cut rubber (above). The broadest emerald green ribbons are made by using (a); the smaller ribbons by using (c); broad parallel lines are made by using (b); and the inner ring of fine lines are created with a date stamp. The four panels and two drawer fronts were treated with the malachite method to accentuate the gothic shape of the panels, thus giving them a jewel-like, stained-glass quality.

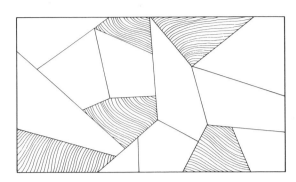

DIVISION OF MALACHITE VENEERS

The surface you are going to work on must be divided up into irregular shapes to resemble veneers (see illustration). To ensure that you have really straight lines use masking tape, only blinding off sections which do not touch each other. Be warned that you take the risk of peeling off the paint when lifting, which is why the underneath paint must be really dry. The principle is exactly the same as the slab method described above, only on a smaller portion each time. Start by painting your dark green onto all the masked sections. Immediately you have malachited each piece, lift off all the tape. Let this dry for 24 hours, then finish off all the rest. After drying go round the veneered sections further separating them with a sharp black line, using a picture frame for guidance. After the top is completely dry varnish with several coats.

Half-round Table

When I moved house, the minute I had seen the place I hankered after, I started to make room plans. The idea was to be able to fit all my beloved furniture into the different spaces and sizes of the new house. Something I have never understood is that on moving from a spacious 'four up and down', to what appeared to be an even larger and more spacious four floors, I ended up having to play God with what had to be sold and what kept, ending up with the sale of quite a few prized pieces I had sweated blood to obtain!

I had imagined everything in place, furniturewise, before I even moved so it was somewhat of a shock to discover that there was an enormous beam, obviously immoveable, in the drawing room which supported the whole house. I waited patiently for two years, hoping to find a reproduction table to match the antique one I had for the far side of the fireplace and eventually had to have one made. My cabinet maker copied a George III table which was made quite a bit smaller to fit the space.

Painting the Table
Materials Needed

* Wood filler
* Squirrel mop brush
* Smaller brushes for rose pattern
* Paint: black emulsion, coloured paints for roses, leaves, etc.
* Beeswax furniture polish
* Liquid polish

Method

Always prepare a new piece by filling, sanding and generally giving it a good clean. Prime and undercoat if you want. I usually do not. Then apply several coats of black emulsion paint with a squirrel mop brush. I could not live without this wonderful tool which leaves no brush marks, if not overloaded with paint. Sand between coats. Now it's time for the fun. I was at great pains not to make a facsimile of the original table, as they would be standing very close to each other, and were already in body the same shape. It is much more subtle to make it appear an accident that you found such a near-matching piece, so in this case I deliberately painted freehand swags of flowers, pink roses, leaves, etc. instead of the more formal Adam flutes, flags and flowers in the deep reds and beiges of the original table. Seal with two coats of liquid polish, then polish with beeswax. There is a saying in the antique trade about a way of faking age: polish your piece once a day for a week, once a week for a month and once a month for a year.

(Right) Half-round or pier table. This is the same shape as a D End which is normally a pair of tables either joined together and used as a round table or, in Georgian times, clipped on to each end of an oblong table.

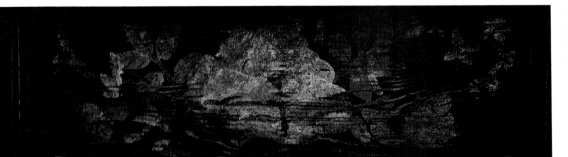

(Left) A detail of the painting on the apron which is a decorative addition to a table either to secure or to hide the top of the legs.

German Cupboard

To my utter amazement, I walked into a local saleroom one day to discover a very similar piece of furniture to my own treasured secretaire (see page 34). It was, in fact a Victorian copy of a seventeenth-century piece. Of course, it was irresistible to me so I put my hand up in the auction, bidding yet again. Everyone in the trade laughed at me because its black and tan appearance was so horrendous. 'Wait and see the transformation', I said, but they still laughed.

I did some research into the style and decided my new acquisition needed its feet put back, so I paid a visit to the local wood turner to order a set of bun feet. In the meantime I got on with the painting. I thought that because the piece was so exotic in itself, a French grey-green antiqued finish would be most suitable for the main body. I wasn't sure what to do with the four panels and two drawer fronts. This often happens, but usually an idea comes to mind while painting the rest of the piece, which can virtually dictate the style. Here I felt that, although the cupboard was already covered in carved cherubs and acanthus leaves, the malachite would enhance the Gothic-shaped panels, giving them a jewel-like quality.

Materials Needed

* Squirrel mop brush
* Grey-green paint
* Watery grey antiquing paint
* Materials as for malachiting (page 85)

Method

Mix enough grey-green, or French green as I call it, paint for the piece. Apply this with the squirrel mop brush. Do make certain that you get into all the carved crevices. When it has dried, antique the cupboard with a watery grey dirty paint (instead of the usual brown). Again make sure it is worked into the exotic carving, lifting off the paint on the high points, to accentuate the design of the piece.

Use the malachite technique described on page 85 to paint the drawer fronts and panels.

Bathroom Sink Unit with Matching Mirror

For some twelve years I told myself that one does not live in the bathroom so it does not need to be huge. At that time mine was 6ft × 4ft (1.8m × 1.2m) so I suppose I would think up some logical reason as a palliative! Of course, on moving house the uppermost thing in my mind was to reverse the situation. My new bathroom measured 12ft × 10ft (4m × 3m) so for the first time ever I had a lovely time choosing all the unusual things one may be tempted to put in such a room. My budget was spread rather thinly over the whole house, so when I was given a beautiful hand-painted Victorian loo, I gratefully used this to set the scene. I then found a freestanding bath from a local council estate which was being modernized. As chance would have it, I found the washstand in the local junk shop, minus its marble top, and decided that would be the grand piece with a bit of tarting up! This is how it was done.

First of all, a new top had to be cut out of blockboard and put on. The drawer was missing from the front so that was blocked up as though it had never been. The feet were missing but replaced from odds and ends kept in one of my many cardboard boxes. To add a bit of style to my humble Victorian piece, I proceeded to use Dutch metal leaf (see page 82) on the curved front legs, making sure it was thoroughly antiqued. Coming across some rather exotic gilded carving in yet another box, this was attached to the front stretcher. The mirror I found had been a picture frame so I painted and Dutch-metalled it to match.

What luxury at last! Until, lounging in the bath one evening in the finished room with a glass of wine, I leaned back to admire my handiwork and was confronted by copper pipes. Horrors! The whole effect was spoilt. So I converted a calico blind into a bag, making the washstand appear like an embroidery work table. The day was saved!

The sink unit depicted here is a Victorian console table normally used with a marble top in a hallway. I find it an extremely elegant piece, easily adapted to its present use. At one time you could pick these pieces up for next to nothing but now they are expensive and difficult to find. The gilded carving under the top was an extra find from a second-hand shop which I added afterwards. The bag was added in order to disguise the pipes but was left open at the back to allow easy access for the plumber.

The arrangement of tulips in an antique blue vase placed on a marble foreground is based on one of my paintings. (Opposite) A baby rabbit hopping through young lettuce leaves. A swan swimming down the Itchen River in Hampshire amongst reeds and water weed. A hare sitting in a field of buttercups and daisies.

Cutouts or Companions

Cutouts or companions, as they were commonly known from about the seventeenth century onwards, were flat, wooden figures of either people or animals. These were placed as decorative and humorous statuettes around the house. The animals did not need looking after and did not suffer from fleas! In more recent years these art forms have again taken their place in fashion. The figures are cut out in fibre board which should be about ¼in (6mm) thick.

There is a choice of stand. The more usual easel stand is a stick of wood, attached to the back of the cutout by a hinge. Or you can use two separate cutouts of flowers and leaves with slits into which the main cutout is slipped, one at each end. (See diagrams.)

Materials Needed

* Fibre board (at least ¼in (6mm) thick)
* Lining paper for walls (grade 800)
* Charcoal
* Blunt implement (e.g. rolling pin)
* Jigsaw
* Sandpaper and wood filler
* Paint: white emulsion, colours suitable for your design
* Spray polyurethane
* Antiquing 'dirty dishwater'

Method

Until you have got used to drawing up a design straight on to the board, draw the shape with charcoal on to lining paper. Place the paper charcoal-side down on the board and press out the pattern with a blunt implement. Go over your outline when the paper has been lifted. Cut out the shape with a jigsaw, keeping the original for re-use. Sand and fill the edges of the board. Apply two coats of white base paint and leave to dry. Re-draw the details freehand or using the pressing method, already described.

Now is the time to paint your design: cat, rabbit, swan, or whatever you have chosen.

If you want it to look old, either use the dirty dishwater paint method or sand it off, or both. You can also cut out separate flowers and leaves, paint them and stick them to the main body of the cutout, giving a three-dimensional look, as I have done with the swan. When the companion is dry, seal it with spray polyurethane so that dusting is easier.

If you use the cutout stand, you can paint a different companion on each side of the board, turning it occasionally to see the other side, or placing it in front of a mirror so that you have two picture views at once, e.g. I painted a Siamese cat on one side, on the other a ginger cat.

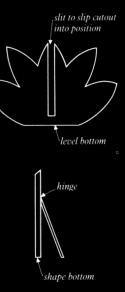

slit to slip cutout into position

level bottom

hinge

shape bottom

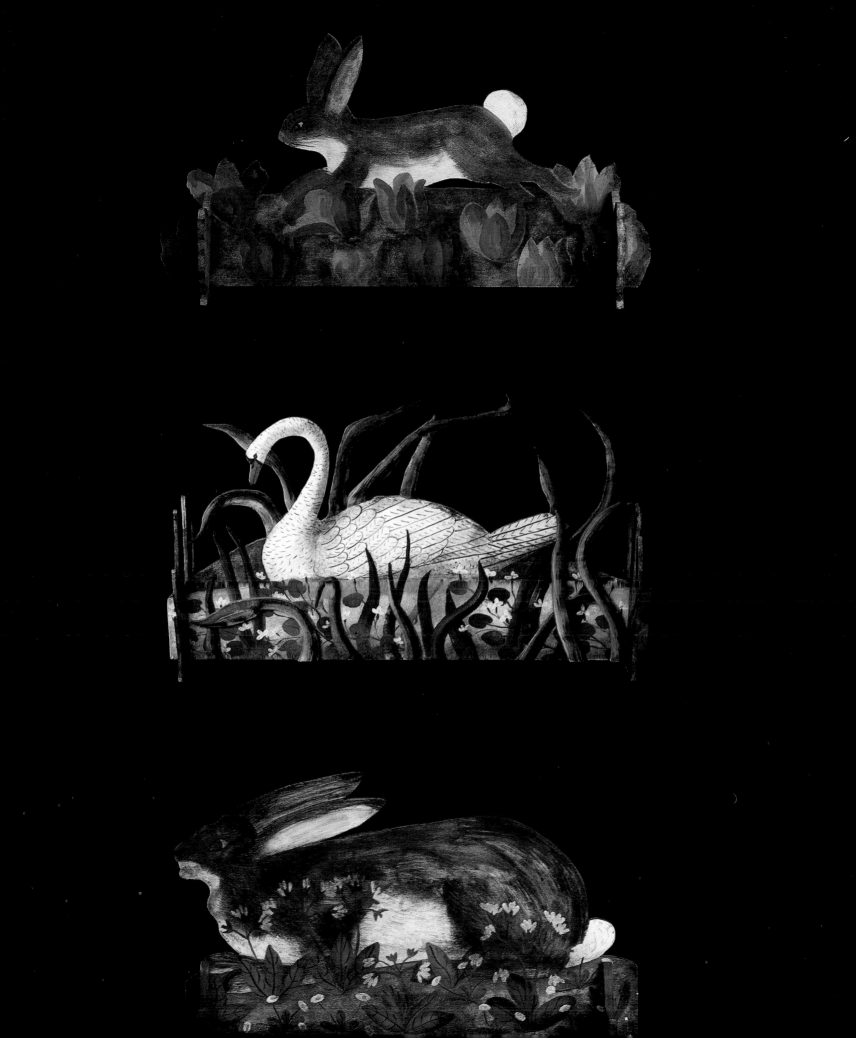

Frames

On one of my many visits to Montacute House in Somerset, I noticed a large quantity of seventeenth-century paintings on loan from the Royal Collection. The frames were wonderfully decorated with gilded leaves and intricate designs. The framing I was using at the time did not permit decorative designs to be applied but, as soon as I had used up my stock, I designed a new sort of frame so that decoration could be painted in the flat middle area of 2in–4in (5cm–10cm).

At first I was rather timid, only applying tentative, rather worn and faded gold lining. People seemed to prefer the black without the gold so only a few frames were decorated. Then I decided to go over the top with gold powders and acanthus-leaf stencils on pictures which I intended to keep for myself. After a couple of years, more and more clients began to ask for their frames to be treated in the same way and some actually began asking for malachite and similar finishes to be done.

Here are some examples of what you can do to enhance a plain picture or mirror frame. Such finishes can add grandeur, not only to the picture, but also to the whole room.

Materials Needed

* Materials for stencilling: stencilling paper, pencil, knife, board for cutting
* Materials for gold powder technique (pages 83 and 85)
* Button polish
* Stiff oil paint brush

Method

Prepare the frame by filling and sanding it thoroughly, then apply two or more coats of emulsion. I always choose black but you can use any colour you like. Draw and cut the stencils as explained on page 73. Mix the gold powders as described on page 85. Stencil with a stiff brush, using stabbing movements.

Let the gold dry thoroughly and antique to taste. (Usually, I antique quite heavily, leaving gold flecks to sparkle through at random, just like real gold leaf.)

There is no need to seal the frame after antiquing if you require a dull look, as the paint is quite strong enough to withstand the amount of normal dusting. Well, it does in my house! My dusting method is to use a soft dustpan brush so that no lint or smears are left behind.

These frames all show variations on the acanthus leaf design with the exception of the frame on the outside edge which has flat, lozenge-shaped leaves, and the one at the very centre which shows a bay or laurel leaf design. These provide variety when one has several pictures hanging adjacent to one another. Any favourite design motif can be applied using gold powders, although acanthus leaves are generally used in classical designs for gilded frames. All the designs are stencils, so one does not have to worry about achieving accuracy in each corner.

Textiles

Cloth has throughout the ages been highly valued. In some parts of the world – Nigeria, for example – the same production methods as practised in ancient Egypt are still used: chewing fibres, then spinning, dyeing and weaving them into rough, heavy, leather-like cloth. Tapa cloth made in Fiji is also chewed, then pressed out, making a paper-like textile on which to paint designs. The cloths I use are mainly antique or calico, often dyed or hand-painted to complement the furniture and wall coverings or to emulate the styles of period decoration. Cloth is one of the most versatile of man-made articles and, with the addition of textiles, simple surroundings can become exotic.

Close-up of a dining area. The rather dramatic effect is created with antique curtains in black and white stripes, echoed by a double sheet which was the only black and white striped fabric I could find at the time. The hand-painted curtain covers the door to the courtyard; when drawn one still has the illusion of a room with a view. Note that the chairbacks are marbled using the black and white marbling recipe (see page 64).

New and Old

The aim with all cloth used in my schemes is to achieve the look of the faded overblown rose, slightly decayed, as with the walls and furniture. I often paint my cloth in order to achieve this mood, but it is important that the base colour under the painting should be realistically 'old' looking. Sometimes I extend the base colour used on the walls to the curtains, which gives you a different tone because the cloth absorbs the pigments more deeply.

The type of cloth I would like to use is so expensive when new, that I use masses of calico instead. I hand paint it with the base colour, leave to dry, then add on the design, using a slightly thicker consistency of paint. Although the paint does not fade, this effect can be established by using the same antiquing methods as for the walls (page 61), or simply mixing your paints in rather dulled (earth) colours.

If using velvets for upholstery, in my case often second-hand curtains, these can be dyed with 'Wash and Dye' in the machine. After only a few months it fades very successfully, thus harmonizing with the rest of the slightly tatty room.

Buying Second-hand

For some years I have combed second-hand shops and salerooms looking for velvet curtains, braids and tassels to enhance my house. Silks are often perfectly sturdy if you are going to use them for curtains, but too old to be used for upholstery.

When buying second-hand materials, be warned that if they smell musty, they will certainly have been damp and any amount of dry-cleaning may not get rid of the smell. Hanging them in the breeze (but not bright sunlight) can help. Do not buy curtains that are 'past it', that is to say, obviously rotten. You can test this by gently pulling the cloth between both hands. Don't pull on the edges of curtains where they may have been exposed to light and sun, only in the middle bottom section.

Preparing and Dyeing Cloth Prior to Painting

After buying your curtains, get the scissors out. Cut off the hem and heading, rip out the lining and give them a good shake.

For dyeing, I use an ordinary powder dye which can be put in the washing machine, following the instructions on quantities (the

more dye you use, the stronger the colour). I dye the curtains one at a time, remembering exactly how many packets of dye were used for each item to be sure of getting the correct shade throughout.

In my experience, most colours can be dyed blue or black. Do not buy red or maroon if you want green: you will end up with brown, and remember that you can never dye a dark colour to achieve a lighter shade.

Hang the cloth out to dry. If you want it to fade, put it in strong sunlight, although I never bother as cloth fades and wears quite quickly in the normal course of events. You should iron the cloth while it is still damp, as the stretching will not always remove the creases. Velvet can be ironed either on a special velvet pad, which looks like a bed of nails, or else put a towel on the ironing board, place the velvet wrong side up over the towel and start ironing away. The pile should come out smooth and perfect.

If you want to use modern chintz, try my antiquing method (see below), as it is difficult to find old chintz in any quantity and, in any case, second-hand chintz is only suitable for curtaining as it is usually pretty worn out. I don't like to bleach cloth. It's rather a drastic step and shortens the life quite considerably as it eventually rots the fibres. Modern dyes are mostly impervious to bleach and sunlight anyway. The method I would favour is either to mix up a generous brew of tea – somewhat absurd for large quantities of cloth. I would normally paint it.

(Above) Victorian copy of a seventeenth-century chair. This was my first attempt at re-upholstering using antique blue velvet and old silver braid. I had the matching stool made and then upholstered it.

(Opposite) It took me three years to prise these antique quilted bedcovers in gold bullion thread off my mother, which I then made into curtains. I hand painted the blind with its inverted pleat to match, using calico.

98

Painting Cloth to Look Old (Chintz or Cotton-based Cloth Only)

Use a large table, or if you have not got one, a sheet of blockboard on trestles or a couple of small tables. Lay out the cloth as smoothly as possible. Square up and put masking tape into place (for curtains, cushions and blinds). Mix up a very watery solution of paint in a browny colour – a 'dirty dish-washer' colour is ideal. With a clean car sponge quickly apply this watery substance by immersing the sponge in the paint, squeezing it out – leaving it fairly wet, and working over the area evenly. Try not to let your paint line dry out, or you will run the risk of having a horizontal mark running over the cloth. I would suggest that if you are making curtains, you cut the cloth first into the finished lengths. Allow for hem and headings.

The result of all this hard work should be a slight dulling and fading which will soften the whole design. When washing, it is better not to spin the cloth unless you want the paint to crack. If you *do*, for the best result, set the machine on high rinse and spin.

I usually wash all painted cloth (curtains and blinds) in the bath. I don't wring them out but transport in a bucket to an upstairs window and hang them out to dry. Because you are using emulsion paint for this process, the colour should not come out when you wash the cloth (on average once a year).

Adirẹ Cloth

Adirẹ cloth, which comes from the Yoruba region and Kano, has always been one of my favourite designs. Due to the difficulty of procuring the real thing, I came across a method to reproduce a similar effect (see p. 128).

I often use these designs painted on tiles and cloth to complement the walls, sometimes in more than one room to tie the general effect together and lead the eye from one area of the house to another. These designs have been used here as hand-painted curtaining and tiles but, of course, could just as well be applied to dados.

All the Adirẹ techniques are 'resist' techniques. Cloth painting and dyeing is a cottage industry in western Nigeria mainly practised in the townships of Ibadan, Oshogbo and Abeokuta. Farming and weaving are the occupations of the men in western Nigeria, but the actual designing and painting, or tying and dyeing of the cloth is done by the women. In the north, however, the dyeing is up to the men. New cloth is used as well as old, shabby lappas which need renewing. (A

(Left) Hand-painted Italian palazzo balustrading with a formal urn and baytree in the foreground applied to calico.

(Below) Adirẹ cloth purchased in Nigeria using the traditional wax and indigo method.

All three designs shown here have been directly influenced by the traditional Adirẹ cloth. The two on the right were done in black and white on to cloth and the one below has been adapted for geometrically patterned wall tiles.

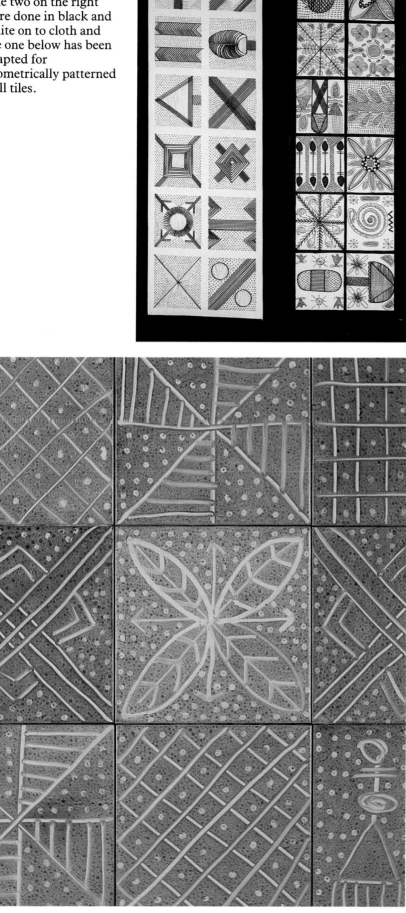

lappa is a cloth up to ten feet long, used to wrap round the body to just above waist level.) Most of the dyeing was carried out on hand-woven cloth until the missionaries introduced calico (probably imported from England or India). In the last few years, modern cloths such as shirting, poplin, velvet and brocade have been used. The indigo pits have been replaced by more modern methods and the dyes by, for instance, Drummer dye or Dylon, as these are quicker and the dyers don't need to be so skilled in gauging (by sniffing) the length of time needed to 'marinate' the cloth in indigo.

Adirẹ eleso

This was produced by taking small portions of the flat cloth and tying in seeds of any shape firmly with raffia. When untied they had created a lozenge shaped design. The seeds were used over and over again.

Adirẹ elelo

In this method the centre of the material was pulled into a peak and the cloth twisted round and round until it had become a cone shape. It was then bound tightly with cotton or raffia.

Adirẹ elesun

This is an offshoot of eleso. The cloth is pleated and sewn up on the pleat with needle and cotton or raffia. The needles were usually made in different sizes by local blacksmiths and different patterns can be produced by using these needles according to the thickness of the woven cloth.

Adirẹ elẹko or batik

This method came after the importation of calico. The pattern was painted with cornflour or starch paste from the cassava plant, with a feather or stick. As time went on, the Abeokuta people made improvements in producing their designs with the use of stencils made from perforated zinc or sheet tin, with simple designs of animals, birds and contemporary people. Many designs depicted historical events such as the Coronation of George V. The designer had greater freedom with this new method, rubbing paste through the stencil on to the cloth. The starch stops the dye from penetrating the cloth to its full extent, so you end up with a pale blue design on a dark blue ground. (The indigo gives a very intense colour.)

In western Nigeria the women use large earthenware dye pots sunk into the ground, while in the North the dye is used in deep cement-lined pits. These are kept covered with conical grass lids, resembling enormous sun hats. The plants used for dyeing in western Nigeria are a species of *Loncho carpus* (a climbing shrub) called Elu in Yoruba, and the mordant (fixative) is the salt in wood ash which is obtained by dripping water through it.

Hand-painted Curtains or Blinds

Materials Needed

* Calico
* Tape measure
* Blockboard or other flat surface
* Fitch
* Mixing bowl for paint
* Black and white emulsion paint
* Natural sponge

Method

First of all, measure out the right amount of calico for the cushion or blind. Then, using masking tape, square the cloth up and hold it down on a piece of hardboard or any other flat surface so that the cloth does not wrinkle or become misshapen during painting. Draw up your design using charcoal or pencil, then mix up the emulsion paint to a creamy consistency. You will need to experiment first on an offcut of the same material to ascertain how the paint will react to the cloth. Adjust the consistency of the paint to suit. Don't be surprised when the paint flowers (spreads) to unexpected places. With practice, you will know how to control the paint so that it doesn't bleed over the edges of the design.

It is advisable not to paint sections next to each other while the paint is still wet, or they may well run in to each other. Leave the paint to dry thoroughly. You can either leave the cloth as it is, or you can antique it by putting it in the washing machine on a long rinse spin, which will make the paint look slightly worn. Where the cloth creases, paler lines will appear. Alternatively, treat with the 'dirty dishwater' method (see page 61).

The front of the curtains can be painted in a marble effect, as shown here. Put the calico into the washing machine on spin rinse. After you've taken it out, lay the cloth onto a flat surface, pulling out the creases as much as possible. (You don't have to secure with masking tape.) While still damp, paint your watery mixture of mid-grey emulsion onto the cloth with a car sponge. Add random darker areas to taste. These subtly blend because the cloth is wet. Immediately, using

a very dark grey or black emulsion (creamy consistency), apply the marbling streaks with a fitch. The lines will 'fizz' out becoming blurred and faded. Dip a natural sponge into the paint mix and scatter black blotches in the vicinity of your streaks by tapping lightly on the cloth. Leave to dry.

Roller Blinds

These are done in the same manner as the curtains, although you will have to test the paint consistency again, as the absorbent quality of the cloth will be different because of the dressing. The edges of blinds have a tendency to undulate when painted, but they will smooth out with use. If using a DIY blind kit, paint and then cut the blind before attaching it to the roller in the normal way.

(Above) Grey and pink marbled design hand-painted on to calico curtains and a blind with an inverted pleat painted in the background colours of the marbling.

(Opposite, top left) Tree of Life design showing detail with birds.
(Opposite, top right) Chinese water lily design in varying shades of green.
(Opposite, below left) Butterflies scattered over a plain white roller blind.
(Opposite, below right) Cyclamen in a blue and white vase, again painted on to a plain white blind.

Gimps

Gimp is a woven cord and braid is flat. Both are used for finishing off upholstered furniture or simply as added decoration. If you cannot find old gimps in enough quantity, you will have to buy them new and 'age' them. The best way to do this is by using tea to give them a faded appearance. Immerse the gimp in cold water, making sure it is totally wet so that the colour will take evenly. Fill a saucepan with water. Put in about four or five Indian tea bags. Stir until the water becomes coloured by the tea then place the wet gimp in the saucepan and simmer just off the boil. 'Cook' for about half an hour. To test whether it is dark enough, cut off a small piece and iron it dry. If it is not as dark as you want, either add more tea or leave to simmer until it is ready.

When you have finished, empty the saucepan into the sink and allow the excess water to drain out of the gimps. It will be very hot so do *not* try to pick it up in your fingers, as I once did, and burnt myself quite badly. Use a pair of spaghetti tongs. Don't run cold water over the gimp or it may shrink. Lay out flat to dry. If you are in a frantic hurry, iron dry at medium heat. Wrap it around a card or stiff envelope to keep it straight; use masking tape on the ends to stop it unravelling.

Tassels

The tea method can be used on new tassels. Do not heat them as you may destroy the wood or card which is the base beneath all silk or wool tassels.

Ink works very well as a black or blue dye for tassels. Mix the ink in cold water. Dip the tassels into the bowl and leave to soak until they have taken up the colour. I have never tried red or other colours, so could not vouch for their success. Although the colour of the dried tassels may seem rather bright at first, the ink certainly fades quickly. Otherwise, for an instant antiqued result, use cold tea.

Braid

I always keep leftover braids and gimps for future use on decorative cushions. Gold braid, sometimes referred to as bullion, should be guarded closely too, as not only is the new stuff extremely costly, it is also rather bright and seems to take forever to tone down. Ends of bolster cushions or small oblong cushions can be made to look more exotic when edged with leftover braid. If you have only a small amount of braid, which would not be enough to edge the cushion, place two vertical strips of braid approximately 3in (7.5cm) from each end of the cushion.

Identification of Historical Textiles

Since textiles can make or break an otherwise successful room, it does help to recognize some of the traditional material and how it was used. This short glossary gives an idea of what sort of cloth to use and where.

Most of these materials are available today but the trouble with modern versions is that the composition may have altered to include man-made fibres which, of course, do not dye as easily or they may have a sheen which is not true to the original look, e.g. cotton velvet versus Dralon, which I never use. Modern factory dyes are specifically formulated not to fade which is another disadvantage since fading is a good way of achieving a realistic effect.

Harrantine

This cloth was a kind of linen used for draping beds in the eighteenth century. It was also used for folding screens.

Mohair

Used in the seventeenth and eighteenth centuries for upholstery and hangings. It was originally made out of the hair of the angora goat, brought into Spain by the Moors. Latterly, the material was made of pure silk.

Counterpane or counterpoint

This was the common term for a cloth bedcover sewn on both sides. From the seventeenth century onwards it was usually made to match the other bed hangings.

Taffety or taffeta

Taffeta was a plain woven material of silk or linen which was also put to general use amongst bed hangings.

Chintz or chint

A cotton cloth used from the Middle Ages onwards, it was usually painted or printed in colours using fast dyes. During the seventeenth century chintzes and painted calicos were being imported to England in great quantity by the East India Company. Subsequently, of course, most of them were manufactured in England.

Any favourite design can be transposed on to a plain white roller blind. Either draw freehand in pencil or chalk or use a stencil.

Cloth of gold or silver tissue

This cloth was introduced to Britain from Spain and Italy. Often a web of silk was used but the most costly cloth was made almost entirely of gold or silver. Where the tissue was made in various colours, crimson, or purple, say, silk was the predominant fibre.

Velvet

Velvet has an even pile, but in times gone by the pile was sometimes left looped (uncut). A method was also used of building up the pile by using different lengths or double pile by introducing silk brocade, sometimes with a gold tissue ground. Genoa and Florence were the earliest recorded manufacturers, from the thirteenth century, and their velvet was highly prized. In the sixteenth century Holland and Bruges had a good reputation for their velvet which used gold threads. Velvet is still produced there for export to Africa where it is sold for a minor fortune, being very highly regarded by the Nigerian Chiefs.

I find second-hand curtains do very well and can easily be dyed and then placed in sunlight to fade quite quickly. When buying modern velvet for dyeing or fading, it is best to choose cotton velvet which does not have man-made fibres included in its make-up.

Plush

This is very similar to velvet but has a much longer pile or nap. Most kinds of natural fibre – cotton, silk or wool – are used in the manufacture of plush, which became fashionable in the early eighteenth century.

All the cloth used here is antique with the exception of the curtains which are hand-painted calico. The bedcover was embroidered circa 1860 and the cushions are made from old velvets and odd leftovers of woollen braids and tassels. The bolster is covered with Thai embroidery done in high relief. The canopy of the Charles II four-poster bed is made from a pair of heavily braided velvet curtains.

Design Resources

For centuries, everyone has been copying everyone else. That is why the well-known designers of clothes, furniture, cloth and wallpapers will often not even talk about what they do in case someone picks up an idea and brings the design into production before the originator can. This chapter gives ideas of what can be achieved with paint used on many different surfaces and shows how the ideas can be taken from sources as varied as Chinese cups and plates and old embroidered tapestry hangings. Of course, nature is the greatest source of design and, as my teacher always reminded me, one should get into the habit of looking above eye level.

Having spent most of my early life in Nigeria, I longed to recreate a wildly exotic jungle scene which took the form of an enormous mural commissioned by a client. The palm fronds, as with all the other plants, had to be painted in their entirety one on top of the other to effect a basketweave of leaves. The flame-of-the-forest flowers are one of my favourites, as they always shaded our verandahs in Africa.

Finding Inspiration

The main idea when decorating a room is to create a theme which enhances your furniture, producing, in my case, an exotic world, with all the necessities of life, such as heating and electricity, camouflaged. The idea of a mural, in my opinion, is to create an illusion. There should be enough interest in the design so that you do not get bored with gazing at the painted walls. I have taken inspiration for my paintings and designs from all over the world. It is very helpful to have photographs and make sketches of interesting patterns, scenes, architecture and landscapes wherever you go.

I am never quite sure in my own mind where a wall decoration stops and a mural begins. I think of a mural as pictorial rather than just a wall design, but I don't always know what category my own paintings fall into. In my own home, my bathroom could be classified as a mural: where you might suppose you are on some shaded Italian roof, looking over distant hills and space (see page 69).

The jungle scenes fall between two stools, being at once exotic designs, having a three-dimensional effect. Those I have travelled in were ragged and often rather dusty, like worn-out stage sets.

Some of my paintings are based on African Mbari houses which are decorated with mud sculptures and also incorporate figures and geometric designs. When I lived in Nigeria, my paintings were mostly scenes from everyday life. Although the jungle and exotic plants were often only depicted as a backdrop, this was later to enable me to design and paint murals based on the scenery I had lived amongst for years.

The Jungle

In Nigeria I always painted in oils, using a palette knife instead of brushes. Of course with oils any errors can be quickly corrected by scraping off the paint. On changing to thin water-based paints and acrylic, I had to learn brush control, along with the restriction of trying never to make mistakes. As you will see on learning my techniques, making mistakes can create problems. I have found it is a good idea to practise for some time on sheets of lining paper, masking-taped together on the back. This is cheap paper so you can use and discard any amount. The method I use is over-painting. For example, when painting a palm tree or banana palm, I

(Opposite) The Persian carpet tiles were originally done to be used on my bathroom floor before I found out that the tiles I had painted were not sufficiently heavy duty for floor use. I have tried to give the feel of the actual pile of the carpet which involved a very laborious 'dabbing' action with a stiff brush. The faded areas show where the wool was hand-dyed.

(Left) A simple example that I thought would be easy to copy if you wanted to recreate the jungle mural. From this basic design you can add as much or as little as you wish.

paint the whole tree, let it dry, then paint the next plant, finger leaf or whatever, on top. The end result gives a better three-dimensional feeling, letting the eye travel into, rather than looking at, the mural. I try to be botanically correct when painting plants, as someone is bound to criticize my artistic licence. At least if you have got the plant correct, they can only complain about the style!

Finding pictures of the plants is not as easy as I imagined. Henri Rousseau, the French artist who painted marvellous primitive jungle scenes at the turn of the century, was of no use at all to me since he had not actually seen many of the things he painted. The best books seem to be those on indoor plant care, which give detailed close-ups and, if you are lucky, may even have a small illustration of the complete plant. You may not feel that you could ever attempt this jungle, but I have given you a simplified drawing of one of the leaves to whet your appetite.

Chinese Water Lily

This design was influenced by a Chinese bowl. The design was never used until I was asked to paint a roller blind for a marble-lined bathroom in shades of green.

Materials Needed

* Chalk
* Stencil paper, cutting
* Car sponge
* Natural sponge
* Face sponge
* Sable pencil brush, nos. 3 or 4
* Small squirrel fan brush
* Chinese brush for stems (medium brush)
* Black and white emulsion
* Powders: ultramarine or cobalt; viridian; chrome yellow; yellow ochre; crimson lake

Method

The design can either be drawn freehand or stencilled on. Prepare the surface in the normal way. Mix up a very thin sky blue, using ultramarine or cobalt blue, white and a touch of black. Apply the paint in a similar fashion to the method described for battered French (see page 64) and leave to dry.

While you wait, cut out the stencils (see page 73), mix up several different shades of green, going from light to dark, using viridian, black, chrome yellow and yellow ochre.

Draw the lines of all the hills with chalk, as shown in the photograph, and fill them in with various shades of green so that each one

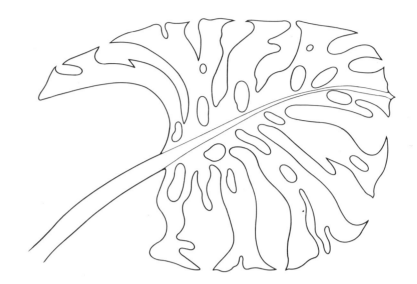

DETAIL OF FINGER LEAF PLANT

is clearly defined, some lighter than others.

Using the stencil, apply the curly shapes to represent water weeds. Stencil the weeds in a fairly dark shade of green, because they are below water level. Cut the stencils of the leaves of the water lily (pages 138–9). You will see that they are darker towards the centre so stencil using a lighter green over the entire leaf. Lift off the wet paint near the edges with a damp face sponge to create lighter areas. Then, with the small sponge, apply shading in the centre of each leaf. The underside of every leaf should be yellow ochre, but the stems are the same colour as the leaf tops. Allow the leaves to dry.

Hand-paint or stencil each flower in white or pale pink. A lovely colour can be mixed using white with a little crimson lake added.

Once these have dried, using the dark green of the leaf, fill in the flower seed pod. Then, using the squirrel fan brush, which makes little lines, paint the stamens in black, dotting the brush at the ends to give a slightly fuzzy effect, indicating the little pollen heads.

Now you can hand-paint the stems to the leaves and the flowers, adding extra tendrils. Make sure all the stems bend and flow into the clumps of weed, not just straight up and down. Then comes the boring part: outlining hills, weeds, leaves, stems and seedpods. I would love to suggest a felt pen, but I have tried one, for speed, and the black faded after only a month or two. Having probably put you off, may I say that the design really does need to be outlined and the adding of all the leaf veins makes all the difference.

Mix up a creamy consistency of black paint. Pour on to a saucer. Using a number 3 or 4 pencil brush, go down all the stems, round the hills and weeds, not forgetting the

(Opposite, above) Chinese water-lily design, with half of it antiqued. The right-hand side has been treated with the dirty dishwater method (see page 61). An alternative way of effecting the water-lily design in simpler form is illustrated opposite below, using Egyptian lotus flowers. Again, the right-hand side has been antiqued, this time using the sanding method (see page 61).

112

(Below) Detail from the Tree of Life design used in my bedroom in which I chose not to show birds or the faggoting stitch.

veining on the leaves. The veining is very important in giving the leaves their exotic curling quality.

When the completed design is quite dry, draw a chalk line to indicate the water level. Use the remainder of the blue, adding more black to deepen the shade. With a natural sponge, freckle the colour all over the design up to the line. If you decide to antique the design, either use the sanding or the 'dirty dishwasher' method (page 61).

The Tree of Life

This design is a direct result of the crewel-work embroidery used on the bed hangings in the seventeenth century (see pages 38 and 106). The bathroom painting was the first one I did and I even painted in the faggoting stitch used to join the lengths of linen together, adding the illusion of velvet binding at the top with little rings to hold it in place.

Materials Needed

★ Charcoal
★ Stencil paper, cutting materials, etc.
★ Chalk

★ Paint brushes 1–1½in (2.5–3.5cm) Hamilton's brush or squirrel mop (for the tree trunks and the 'velvet' edging); medium Chinese brush (for the vine tendrils); pencil brush, no. 2 or 3 (for veining leaves and outlining insects, etc.); pipe-over brush (for the ploughed fields)
★ Natural sponge (which fits comfortably in the palm of your hand)
★ Face sponge
★ Black and white emulsion paint
★ Powders: ultramarine and cobalt blue

Method

First of all, mix up a lightish blue and with a natural sponge, paint the area to be 'hung' with your crewel embroidery design. When this is dry, draw on to the wall, using charcoal or chalk, all the hillocks at the base, then the tree trunks. Paint the latter rich blue. The blue is ultramarine or cobalt added to black. As you paint the trunks, sponge off with a damp natural face sponge to highlight one side of the branches. Stop painting the trunks where they meet the hillocks.

Cut out all your stencils. (See page 73 for method and pages 133–5 for stencil shapes.) Now begins the stencilling, which is done in the same blue as the trunks and a mid-blue between the base colour and the dark blue. I make up the design as I go along, adding the curling vine tendrils and stems after I have put all the main attractions into place. Then I fill the gaps with the cherry branches. If you are not confident enough, sketch out a plan of the tree, hillocks etc. beforehand so that you have something to follow. You can even lightly chalk the design on to the wall before you begin painting.

The hills are treated in different ways: some are sponged, others flat-painted or made to look like ploughed fields, using a pipe-over brush. This is a special brush with either three or seven tubes attached to the ferrule (see page 46).

Add butterflies, birds and insects (see pages 136 and 137), and outline them in black.

Again, the boring bit! Use thinned dark blue or black paint and no. 2 or 3 pencil brush for lining and veining all the leaves. Add hatching (criss-cross lines) to some of the flowers or any other decorative line work. You are nearly finished. Let the whole room dry and antique in the usual way (see page 61). Lastly, when you paint the 'velvet' edging at the top of the 'tapestry', use the same method as for the tree trunks. Cut a stencil for the rings, which are painted metal grey.

(Left) Tree of Life design. First used in this bathroom, it became the prototype for later designs. I decided to emulate the hanging-tapestry-look even to the extent of stencilling the faggoting stitch used in the seventeenth century to join lengths of cloth together.

115

Bamboo Wall

This design was created after a visit to Brighton Pavilion, an enormous palace with onion-shaped domes built by the Prince Regent (later George IV) in 1762. The bamboo plant, which had been imported from China, became extremely fashionable in Regency England and great use was made of it in the Pavilion, not only on the walls, but the furniture too.

Although at first glance this mural may look complicated, once you have got the hang of it, my methods are really easy.

Find some examples of living bamboo or paintings on china and furniture. It will make it easier to draw the plant in the stylized manner of the Chinese.

Materials Needed

* Natural car sponge
* Chalk
* Charcoal (optional)
* Squirrel fan brush (small)
* Pencil brushes, nos. 3 and 4
* Fitch
* Terracotta (see colour mix on page 49) emulsion; black and white emulsion
* Powders: ultramarine or cobalt blue; viridian green; chrome yellow; yellow ochre; crimson lake

Method

Mix up a palish terracotta, then water some of the mix down to a milky consistency to do the battered French finish (see page 64). Let it dry. Sponge the undiluted paint in a very open manner to break up the base coat. Leave to dry. With chalk rather than charcoal, draw your hillocks, which should vary in height between 9in and 12in (20cm–30cm), also adding the main stems and leaves of the bamboo.

Mix up a largish quantity of blue-green base colour. Then, by adding small quantities of black, yellow or white to small quantities of the base colour, you can vary the colour of the hillocks, one from another. Then, while the hills are still damp, use the natural sponge on the top line to give a grassy look and soften the hard edge of each mound.

Using the base blue-green, paint the whole leaf and stem. Decide which way the light falls (see page 76), and then apply a darker mix of the base colour to the shade side of the leaves and the stems, using a Chinese brush or fitch, whichever is easiest for you. Before the paint has dried, add the highlighting to the leaves and stems, using a lighter mix of the base colour.

If you look at the example you will see that the leaves have a lined effect where the lighter colour was applied. To achieve this, load a squirrel fan brush with the lighter mix and start at the top of the leaf, placing the brush on its side. Draw the brush in one continuous movement towards the base of the leaf, twisting it so that the hair of the brush lies flat in its fan shape and then returning it to its side three-quarters of the way down the leaf. This gives a broken vertical lined effect not unlike the ridges in a bamboo leaf. You can further enhance the effect by suggesting the shine with a modest quantity of white painted in the same manner.

Mix up a 'squashed caterpillar' colour, adding yellow ochre to the base colour to simulate the dried-up leaf sheaths which protect the leaf before it has opened, and which usually stay attached to the plant for some time. Add a few leafy squiggles at the top of the bamboo stem to suggest new growth.

With a dark mix of blue-green paint or black, outline the bamboo leaves and stems with a fine pencil brush, putting a central vein in each leaf.

When all this has been done, the fun begins with butterflies, which are excellent fillers to balance up any rather bare areas of the wall. If you do not feel confident enough to draw them freehand, you could trace them with a thin stick of charcoal from enlarged photocopies of the examples shown at the end of the book. Then hold the tracing, charcoal-side to wall. Rub the design onto the wall with a blunt implement. But do practise with the freehand drawing. I am certain that if you do, you will be able to manage it.

Once drawn, outline the shape, putting in any details with either the dark green or black. Leave to dry then, with very watery paint, paint in yellow, pinks or pale greens, filling in the wings and letting the darker shapes show through the paint.

The Chinese bamboo design shows two different methods of finish – the left-hand panel is unantiqued while the right-hand section is antiqued using the 'dirty dishwater' technique.

116

Creating a Room Set

Turning an idea into reality should be fun, especially when refurbishing your house. Depending on your ideas for creating a home – whether modern or influenced by times gone by – you will need to start with furniture, perhaps only one piece, which will set you in motion. Then come the months or even years of collecting and choosing cloth, carpets and ornaments. I believe the creation of peace and beauty are most significant in your home. Just as your clothes should not wear you but you should shine above them, so with your home: you are the star and your creation must be the perfect backdrop in which you feel relaxed and at one with your surroundings.

The drawing room illustrates a mélange of new and old, which co-exist perfectly. The Charles II cabinet on a stand is my pride and joy. This is an English example of Chinese lacquer work. The sofa is Indo-Portuguese, highly carved in ebony wood, complemented by antique Turkish embroidery which uses gold bullion thread and the emerald green wings of the scarab beetle to add light refraction. A modern Italian perspex table is used to display a collection of favourite items.

The Focal Point

Most of us cannot afford to start entirely from scratch. There may be pieces which have sentimental value or which would be too expensive to change. These will have to be incorporated into the re-decoration so choose a style which they will be at home in.

Most rooms require a focal point – somewhere for the eye to rest, which pulls the room together. This is usually a fireplace. Where there is no fireplace, a piece of antique or painted furniture serves the same purpose. My own method of planning a layout is aesthetic and practical: for me the aesthetic quality takes precedence over life's practicalities. I would rather have a hand-painted kitchen surface than a heat-proofed finish when I can't find the design I like.

In my small bedroom I overcame the problem of too much furniture and not enough space. I emptied the room so that the four-poster bed and I could shuffle round until the best position was found. Next came the chest of drawers which had to double up as a dressing table. The wardrobe was placed opposite the window and, miraculously, a chair found enough space in the corner.

Although my priority is visual, you must be able to use a room and be comfortable in it.

I give every room this treatment, especially the bathroom, where the plumbing dictates the position of the lavatory. The bath and basin can then be tried in various positions. In fact, my last bathroom was all set out before we put the dividing wall up between the bedroom and the bathroom, with me shouting to the builder, 'Four inches towards the bedroom', until I got the washstand in, which I was simply determined to do at all costs.

A Word About Floors

It is much easier to match paint to floors than flooring to paint, so concentrate first on choosing the floor. Examine all carpets and textiles in daylight and electric light. Colours can change quite dramatically in different lights. Because haircord is woven so does not have a pile, Persian carpets and rugs or throws can be laid onto it without 'walking'.

Final Touches

When all your hard work is done, now is the time to have a good look at the room. Ornaments can make or destroy the whole feel of the room. So great attention should be paid to lighting, door furniture, fire-irons, cushions and curtains.

(Opposite) The Delft rack was purchased in an Oxfam shop and was in a terrible state of disrepair but, after lots of loving care and attention, was restored to its former glory. The freehand border, which is rather covered up by the pictures of auriculas, is known as the wandering grape design.

(Below) Two very different examples of taking marbling to an extreme. The fish picture mounts were revived by marbling them to match the walls they hung on (page 62). The lamp shade was painted to show off the pink marble fire-surround.

(Opposite) The tapestry curtains which frame this window have been used on beds or windows in various surroundings. The blind is hand-painted and 'cracked' by running it through high speed in the washing machine to make it look aged. The panelling underneath enriches the cardinal painting above, glimpsed through the wood-painted-to-look-like wood balustrade.

All the examples you see in this book, both blinds and curtains, are always made at least a foot too long for the window, so that they can be hitched up in any way you like, or just left undraped and crunched up on the floor. It was not until about the 1950s that curtains were hung an inch or so off the floor. Before this curtains were about 2in (5cm) longer than floor length to stop draughts from windows or doors. In my opinion, longer curtains look far more sumptuous and can help a rather plain room appear more elegant.

In bedrooms, bedcovers, valances and even the sheets are part of the plan. I found it difficult to buy patterned sheets which reflected seventeenth-century taste, until I came across some glazed chintz with authentic seventeenth-century designs on it. This made my bed look even more fabulous and although the glaze eventually wears off with washing, the pure cotton lasts and is comfortable to the touch.

Collecting should be fun. Don't buy the first thing you see if it's not what you want because, as sure as eggs is eggs, you'll find the perfect piece round the next corner.

How a Disaster Area with Seven Doorways was Transformed

When I moved into my present abode, I found the back shop (now the entrance hall) was a disaster area. This was one of the few rooms where walls had to be pulled down, the fireplace reinstated, the chimney made larger with a false wall so that it would appear more important, and the staircase remodelled. Walking into the house, you opened the door on to a somewhat squalid passage with a window facing the brick wall of the garage, a door on the right leading into a dark, dingy room and another door to the cellar. The stairs were blocked in with barred windows and there was yet another door next to the cellar door, leading to a downstairs lavatory with no floor!

(Right) The Disaster Area with Seven Doorways after it was transformed. The eighteenth-century ship's cabin columns are holding up the whole structure, which had to be put in between visits from the surveyor! Grizelda lies in the foregound.

123

The garage was my first venue of attack: off with the roof and down with the wall! Ah! fresh air at last. The passage window was taken out to be replaced by a second-hand door and an iron grille off a Russian ship was put over the area to lead into the garden – or what was to become an instant garden. My aunt always said one should plant the garden first so that it could grow while the building work was being done. I have followed her advice for years.

The next stage was to attack the interior, so I pulled down the passage wall, which turned out to be a better idea than I had thought, as mountains of dry rot were lodged securely in the ceiling. The room was vastly improved. But when I moved the furniture into the house, I soon discovered that it would not go up the staircase, so against all advice about fire regulations, I personally pulled the windows and wall down and replaced the supporting timbers with solid mahogany eighteenth-century ship's cabin columns which I had in stock.

I was now left with a room with seven windows and doors, all at different heights and the only things with any architectural merit were the oak fireplace and the columns. To unify the room, I painted dark panelling round the whole area, leaving only the garden as a feature. Being painted brown, the panelling leads the eye straight to the garden.

To try to even up the different heights of doors and windows, I used mountains of cloth. As the windows reach the ceiling, I hung hand-painted calico curtains from ceiling height at all the doors and windows. These were dress curtains only with blinds to shut out all the cold draughts that creep through badly fitting windows. I do not like double-glazing as I feel closed in.

The curtains already gave the room an air of grandeur so I had to be careful not to clutter it up with too much furniture. It is now used as a spare work room when pieces are too large to go up the stairway, or else as a dining room. I keep a folding army table for such occasions, but it is mainly the entrance to the house and garden, so is like a huge passageway for dogs and people alike.

Chinese Room Set

For this room I was asked to design an interior with a distinct Chinese influence, which would fit into a modern or period European house. Since yellow is always evocative of China, being the colour only the Emperors were permitted to wear, I decided to make that the main colour, treating it in

different ways with the use of velvets on the chairs and some original Fortuny curtains I had picked up in my local sale room some two years before. Both cloths give an immediate look of grandeur and are exotic at the same time.

The main influences on the colour for the walls were the yellow glaze vase and the Chinese stool. Normally, I would not have been able to afford either of these, especially the vase because it is very early and in the somewhat rare Chinese Imperial yellow. But the vase is cracked and the stool slightly damaged, which enabled me to purchase them.

The wall design is in the same basic Imperial yellow. I chose to stencil magnolia flowers which are not an unusual sight in our gardens, and happen to be one of my favourite plants. I then hand-painted the trunks and branches. Stencils have been used for the bamboos (introduced, along with the magnolia, from China in the eighteenth and nineteenth centuries when European plant hunting expeditions were in their heyday). The butterflies I used as usual, which were originally inspired by Chinese decorations on plates and vases.

Next, the furniture. The main piece is a black and gilded Chinese lacquered centre table, dating from the early eighteenth century. You will notice that the table top is pink marble which ties in with the blind – a modern, heavy viscose chosen for its echo of the marble on the table. The Georgian chair is upholstered in old yellow velvet and trimmed with silver bullion gimp which I had found in a junk shop and squirrelled away for the right occasion. The stool was made for me by a cabinet maker. It is just for occasional use when there are too many guests, or it can be drawn up to the chair as a footstool for that relaxing afternoon nap. The Persian rug relieves the austerity of the carpet.

Finally, I included my 'Chinese Chippendale' style of fencing on the dado rail, which gave the room continuity.

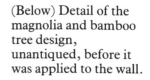

(Below) Detail of the magnolia and bamboo tree design, unantiqued, before it was applied to the wall.

(Opposite) Magnolia and bamboo design showing the dado which is in the Chinese Chippendale style, painted in dark green in the same shade as the bamboo. This whole design has been antiqued with sandpaper to give it a worn look.

Here the magnolia and bamboo design is shown in use in a formal setting. Although I have described the furnishing of this drawing room in detail on page 124, I think you will see how such an exotic idea can transform the most ordinary of rooms into elegant and peaceful surroundings.

African Room Set

All my life I have been surrounded by blue, which is worn by most people in one form or another in Nigeria.

My African room was designed round the pale blue, hand-painted cloth which was influenced by the Nigerian Adiṛẹ cloth. For this room I painted the design onto calico with wax and then sponged on very thinned emulsion paint which cannot penetrate the wax so gives a similar feeling to the traditional faded indigo, but is a much shorter and less complicated process.

Although the chairs are not from Nigeria (they are Indian), they evoke the beaten metalwork done in Kano, the first city after the Sahara Desert and strongly influenced by the Arabs.

The table is a modern one but with a hand-painted top, evoking the mud sculptures from the east of Nigerian Ibo land.

Adding to this style, I have used an antique chief's door, ivory bracelets and a Mummee statue. This room also provides a home for a clay Abuja pot which I bought from a woman near the village for only a few pence and lovingly carried back from the north of Nigeria to the south on my knee in the car. Ayo, a famous gambling game similar to chess and played throughout Nigeria, was a present.

On the floor is marbled linoleum which can have matting, rugs or Persian carpets added for extra comfort and luxury.

The plant has a silvery colouring which goes well with metal and curtains in the room, and looks as though it comes from Africa, even if it doesn't.

The Drawing Room

My drawing room has had an unusual time. Before I came to the house all the decorative details had been ripped out except the ceiling. In fact, that was one of the main reasons that I bought the house; I just loved the room. I liked the plastered ceiling, although it is not very grand compared with some, and imagined it painted to look similar to the sky.

The first thing I did was to strip off the terrible 1920s paper which was not as clean as it might have been and very ordinary. I rushed back to Alresford to buy a fire surround that had been offered to me one year earlier and I had felt was too costly, but with inflation it had become a better deal. I cut 2 feet (610mm) off the width and 5 feet (1.5m) off the height and fitted it to the wall, leaving my decision on the colour until later, as it was originally in the darkest oak.

Before the flood, and after visiting Montacute house in Somerset, I thought that the room should be blue, with the paintwork and fire surround in stone colour. I wanted the ceiling to look like the sky and the day I painted it there was a rain storm. So that is what it resembles, which nobody fails to remark upon. Well, that is what the weather is mostly like in this country, so why pretend? Anyway it is dramatic and has toned down with the constant dust and smoking that goes on year in and out.

Next, I bought some wonderful blue watered silk and painted the walls to match, having replaced the picture rail and the dado rail. I then sat in the room for some six months with water streaming down the walls, whilst my next-door neighbour carried on his building work. He explained that my roof got in the way so he took part of it off. I thought I might lose the ceiling, which was a devastating thought: not only could I not afford to replace the plasterwork of leaves and ribbons, but I had spent many days painting it.

The ceiling survived, but I decided that blue and water were synonymous, so yellow seemed the obvious choice. Thank goodness, the shop accepted the return of their cloth in exchange for the yellow brocade that now takes pride of place at the windows.

It is difficult to know which way round to do things – cloth or walls – if you are using paper. After a great search, I found a style of paper which looked slightly faded and was of similar design to the papers used in the seventeenth century. The dado was influenced by the grand gilded rooms of Ham House and done in yellow ochre and gold powders to simulate gilded acanthus leaves. Believe it or not it was the most tedious part of the house to paint, I would imagine because the stencils get so clogged with the gold powders and button polish.

The furniture, which I already had, is mostly comprised of seventeenth- and eighteenth-century English, with an assortment of international pieces. I still add the occasional piece of porcelain from China when it is cheap enough, which usually means it is less than perfect, as I prefer to have the very early pieces and cannot afford the price of perfection. The paintings also change from time to time but the basic structure of the room remains.

I needed a space in which to place my African collection. The room was created using my hand-painted cloth, heavily influenced from the original Adiṛẹ. The rather intriguing wooden carving under the table is a gambling game known in Nigeria as Ayo.

Epilogue

I hope that having read this book and looked at all the photographs you will feel like tackling some of my techniques. Although the idea of turning your rooms into a fantasy world may look difficult, I can assure you that, once you have started, you will find not only are the methods quite simple but that you evolve your own ways of doing things, often quite by accident.

My attitude to creating rooms is to make the whole thing fun. Although you may start with quite a rigid plan it will change as you go along, which is quite exciting as one is never sure what the end product will turn out to be. This usually comes about because you buy a piece of furniture or a pair of antique curtains which you simply cannot live without, and the design of the room has to take this into account.

Two different aspects of the same room. This is my new look: the stencilled dado and border are Chinese-oriented whilst still using the Adirẹ cloth to enhance the crisp blue and white. Although the blinds are inexpensive – Chinese reed blinds which can be bought anywhere – they were awkward to make up. I first painted the blinds with very thinned emulsion. The borders and heads were then made up of calico stencilled to match the borders on the walls and hand-sewn with a curved upholstery needle which ripped my hands to shreds. The tassles were attached with a looped piece of matching cloth in the manner used in the Far East when the blind was hand-rolled.

When faced with a nice, clean, white room I still get the shakes in clients' houses and have to down some coffee to steady the hand while telling myself that it's only paint and can be re-painted. Sometimes I am filled with horror at the thought of an intricate design which must be repeated many times. In my bedroom, the wall panel was done sixteen times with four different methods to each panel. By the time I had finished one wall I was not too keen to carry on. The alternative was to obliterate several hours of work, or turn up the music, switch on the TV to a 1940s film, and just keep telling myself that it was only a one-off. When it's finished, you realize that it was all worthwhile. After some months I find myself doubting that I actually had the patience to do it – until I start all over again somewhere else.

Do not be afraid to take your design ideas from any source available. Everyone has been copying each other for years and nothing is new. You are personalizing the design and this makes quite a difference as your walls, furniture or cloth will have a fresh approach to an old idea.

Having spent some fifteen years closeted with the illusion of the sixteenth and seventeenth century, some of my friends asked none too politely if my parents worried about me, as it seemed to them a very strange idea to live in another century. They will now be able to comment on my new work which involves the use of stencils to fashion the colonial and Chinese decorative effects which are at present evolving in my house. It is wonderful fun selling all the oak to be replaced by Chinese lacquer or exotic hardwoods from Burma and Thailand. Read all about it in the next book.

Stencils

These stencils all represent design details or motifs which occur throughout the book. To reproduce them, either trace them or photocopy direct from the book and size up accordingly.

The peonies and butterflies on page 132 and the birds and butterflies on pages 136–7 are all taken from the two Chinese dining rooms which use the same stencils with different colourways (see pages 40–1). The birds are also used in the bathroom Tree of Life design (page 114).

On this page (above) you will see leaves from the Tree of Life design which should be used in conjunction with the stencils on page 134 which illustrate three different shapes of grassy tussocks and three tulip plants, all of which grow on the hillocks at the base of the design. Page 135 shows varieties of pinks (the central one is from Persia) on the right of the page and two polyanthus, with

a fantasy flower in the middle, on the left-hand side of the page. The Tree of Life is featured on pages 38, 59, 60, 103, 106–7 and 115–16.

Pages 138 and 139 are for the Chinese Water Lily design, the recipe for which appears in Design Resources on p. 112. Illustrated here are folded and open leaves, seaweed tendrils, seed pods, a budded leaf and lily flowers. It is also featured on pages 59 and 103. Pages 140 and 141 show the magnolia flowers and bamboo which were used in the Chinese yellow room set (pages 124–7). The flowers can also be incorporated into the Chinese style dining room designs (pages 40–1).

Index

acanthus-leaf design 21, *21*, *84*, 95, 128
    on frames *94–5*
    tiled *23*
Adam, Robert 25
Adire cloth 12, 100–1, *100*, *101*
    influence of *101*, 128, *128–9*, *130*
animal designs 53
    as cutouts 92, *93*
    on hangings 25
    on tiles 79
antiquing technique 61, *61*, *80–1*, *117*
    battered French 68
    cloth 98
        chintz 98
    gimp/braid 105
    metal finishes 85
    tiles 77
architecture, painted 57

backgrounds 52, *53*
    on tiles 79
bamboo 116, *116–17*
    Japanese 36, *36*
    and magnolia 124, *124*, *125*, *126–7*
bathrooms 62, 68, 69, 71, 77, *90–1*, *114*, *115*
    planning 120
battered French technique *26–7*, 30, 64–8, *66–7*
    preparing walls for 58
    rectifying mistakes 44
bay/laurel leaf design *94–5*
bedcovers: counterpane 105
    as curtains 99
    painted 25
bedrooms *26–7*, *31*, *31*, *74–5*
    planning 120, 123
beds *31*, *74–5*, *80–1*, *83*, *106–7*
binders 18
bird designs 21, 52
    on hangings 25
    on tiles 77, *78*
    see also Tree of Life
blinds 124
    Chinese reed *130*
    hand-painted *99*, 100, 102, *103*, *104*
        'cracked' *122*
        washing 100
    length of 123
    roller 102, *103*, *104*
blockboard: preparing 71, 72
borders 39
bolster cushion 105, *106–7*
braid 105

Brighton Pavilion *13*, 116
brushes 44
    Chinese *42–3*
        control methods 40
    for marbling 64
    routine when using 47
    for water-based paint *46*, *46–7*
bullion (gold) 25, *26–7*, 99
    on cushions 105
butterfly designs 52, *53*, 116, 124

calabashes *10*
calico 97
    hand-painted *100*, *106–7*
carpets: choosing 120
cast iron: disguising 49, *50*
ceilings, painted *52*
Chambers, Sir William 40
cherub/putto design *52*
Chinese waterlily *112–15*, *113*
chintz 9, 98, 105
    as sheets 123
clapboard 18
cloth: antique 97, *106–7*
    painting technique 100
    preparing and dyeing 98
    second-hand 28, 97, 98
    washing 100
    see also individual types
cloth of gold 107
colours 18, 38
    blue 47, 128
        using 48
    Chinese porcelain 21
    'country house' 32
    earth 48–9
        using 49
    effects: on cloth 98
        on furniture 81
        of sealant on 44
        of varnish on 47
    lightening dark rooms 47
    matching 30, *30*, 31, *31*
    mixing 44, 49
        emerald green 86
        grey 49, 63, 64
        Prussian blue 49
    north-facing room 47, *48*
    onglaze 76, 77
    pastel 21
        on furniture 25
    primary: on furniture 25

softening/blending 31, 47
    using *47–9*
    white: mixing primaries with 49
    yellow 124
columns *24*
    plinth of 18
companions 92, *92–3*
cornices 52, 62
Cotehele House, Cornwall 28
cracks, filling 58
crewel work *26–7*, 28, 52, *114*, 115
    see also Tree of Life
curtains *96–7*, 99, *122*
    dress 124
    hand-painted 25, *96–7*, 97, 98, 100, 102
        washing 100
    length of 123
    second-hand 98
cushions *106–7*
    braid/gimp on 105
    hand-painted 100
cutouts 92, *92–3*

dados 18, 38, *38*, *39*, 52, 124, *125*
    gilded 128
    on large walls 30
    optical illusions 30
    panelled 18, *19*, 21, *21*, *31*, *31*
        measuring for 58, *58*
    stone effect 69
    with battered French walls *66–7*
designs: adapting 40–1, *40–1*
    Chinese 40–1, *40*, *41*, *45*
        dados *39*, 124, *125*
        porcelain 21, *39*, *39*
    freehand *38*, 52
    geometric: Florentine 37, *37*
        on furniture 25
        on panelling 18
    Palladian 21
    sources 28, 52, 109, 110
    see also individual types
dining area *96–7*
dining room 30, *30*, 40–1, *40*, *41*, 62
    detail *45*
'dirty dishwater' technique 45, 61, *61*, *117*
    metalled finishes 85
    tiles 77
doors/doorways *10*, 62, 70, 123, *123–4*
    disguising 30, 40–1, *60*, 61
    paint treatments *60*, 61
    panel decoration *84*

special features for 61, 64, 70
unifying heights 124
dragging technique 41
on doors 60
drawing room 66–7, 118–19, 128
drying agents 18
Dutch metal leaf 82–3, 83, 90, 90–1
dyes/dyeing 98, 105
Adire 100–2
velvet suitable for 107

Edwards and Darly 40
Emokpae, Erahbour 12
emulsion 9, 12–13, 43, 44
effect of light on 44
English oak design 28
equipment 44
see also brushes

fingermarks, removing 47
finishes, textured 49–52
fireplaces 20, 21, 51, 52, 71, 128
as focal point 120
matching materials 62
flame-of-the-forest design 53, 108–9
floors 120
protecting from paint 47
flower designs 25, 32, 32, 33, 112–15, 113, 124,
125, 126–7
cutouts 92, 92
on hangings 25
on tiles 23, 76
see also individual types
frames 94–5, 95, 120
friezes, uninterrupted 40
fruit designs 121
baskets of 32
swags 16, 21
on tiles 76
furniture: choosing 119
copies 28
as focal point 120
painted 80–1, 86
preparing for 82
protecting when decorating 47
restoring 82–90
planning layouts 120
re-upholstered 28, 81, 98
see also individual items

gardens, as feature 124
inspiration from 28, 38
German cupboard 90
German secretaire 34, 35, 86
details 34
gilding technique 21, 21, 82
gimp 105, 124, 126–7
glazes 44
gold powders 83–5, 94–5
gouache 9, 43
mixing 44
thickeners 44
graining technique 25, 59
alternative to 52, 71, 71–2
fantasy 72, 72
grease marks, removing 47

Ham House, Surrey 21, 28, 72, 72, 128
hangings, bed: embroidered 26–7, 38
painted 25
patterns for 25
hangings, wall: protecting 18
harrantine 105
holes, filling 58

Indian flower designs 25
see also Tree of Life design
'instant ancestors' 8, 19

japanning technique 25
Jungle 108–9, 110, 110–12
detail 112

keystones, painted 70, 70
kilns 76
kitchens 68, 71
painted work-surfaces 38, 120

lacquer technique: application of 25
carved 25
Chinese 118–19
on furniture 25
lampshades 120
light, effect on paint 44, 45
lines, painting 30
lotus flowers design 113

magnolia and bamboo design 124, 125, 126–7
detail 124
marbling technique 41, 52, 59, 60, 62, 62–4, 120
applying veins 64
black effect 63, 64
curtains/blinds 102, 102
Egyptian/Roman 18
frames 120
furniture 25, 60, 96–7
grey and white effect 63, 63–4
mouldings 64
rectifying mistakes 44
sources 62–3
tiles 79
marbling feathers 64, 64
medallions: on furniture 25
metal finishes: repairing 82–3
see also individual types
mirrors 19, 28–9
see also frames
mohair 105
Montacute House, Somerset 28
mouldings 64
murals 18, 57, 108–9, 110, 110–12, 116, 116–17
detail 112

ornaments, choosing 120–3
over-painting technique 100–12
on stencils 41, 73

paint 9
consistency 45
for antiquing 45
for curtains/blinds 102
for marbling 63
for sponging 62
for stone effect 69
dulling/ageing 48, 49
mixing 44–5, 48
for 'dirty dishwater' 61
for malachite effect 86
quantities 44–5
for stone effect 69
for wood effect 72
oil-based 18, 43, 44
effect of light on 44
preparing surfaces for 58
removing lumps/skin 45
reproducing tatty 13
see also battered French technique
sense of depth 49–52
water-based 44
drying time 44
effect of light on 44
working with 47
see also binders; drying agents; emulsions;
gouache; powder paint
paintwork, reproducing tatty 13
palampores 25, 28, 38
panelling 30, 30, 31, 31
colour of early 21
Ham House style 122
japanned/lacquered 25
linenfold 18
measuring walls for 58, 58
patterns on 18
Elizabethan 73–4, 73, 74–5

simulated 30, 30
on furniture 25
to unify room 124
wood 18
see also dados: panelled
Persian carpet design 111
Persian flowers 25
Persian tree 22
pigments: preparing 48
pure 44
plasterwork, decorated 21
plush 107
'poor man's gold' 82–3
powder paints 9, 43
mixing 44

radiators 44, 58–61, 59, 72
ragging technique 52
rails 18
repainting, preparation for 44
re-touching 44
Rousseau, Henri 112

sandpaper technique 61
screens, Japanese 36
sealers: for cutouts 92
malachite effect 86
metal leaf 83
over water-based paint 44
semi-precious stone technique:
malachite 60, 61, 85–90, 88, 89, 90–1
details 87
veneer divisions 88
metal leaf in 83
silver tissue 107
size: glue 18
for metal finishes 82
skirting 61, 62
spattering technique 52
on tiles 79
sponges 47
sponging technique 52, 61, 61–2
carved wood 34, 34–5
dry 62
rectifying mistakes 44
tiles 79
sprig designs 31
staining technique 25
stencils 73–6, 132–41
for basic design 40–1
cutting 73
mending 75, 75
using round corners 45, 73
stencilling technique: on frames 94–5, 95
gilded 21, 21
over doorway 64
panelling 73–4, 73–4
shading 76
see also over-painting
stiles 18
stone: substitute 51, 52
stone finish technique 59, 68–70, 69, 70
exterior 56–7, 70
marking 'joints' 69–70
Street, Evelyn 12
stringing 30
styles: African 128, 128–9
Chinese 40–1, 40–1, 124, 125, 126–7
importance of research 28–30
swags 31, 31, 52
on furniture 25

tables 65
taffety/taffeta 105
tassels 105, 130
techniques: practising 110
see also individual techniques
textiles, historical 105–7
tiles 21, 22, 38, 52, 77, 111
complementary 100
painting glazed 76–9

Tiles – *contd.*
  useful sources 28
Tree of Life design 38, *38*, 59, *60*, *114*, 115
  colours for 38
  detail *115*
trompe l'oeil 52, 57
tulip designs 32, *32*, 33

undercoats, oil-based 44

varnishing 47
velvet 107
  ironing 98

wainscot 18
wandering grape design *121*
wax-resist technique *11*
  batik 101
Whistler, Rex 57

window frames 62
window sills: protecting paint on 47
windows: counteracting lack of 69
  unifying heights 124
wood: chips in 47
  cleaning 47
  emulsion on 44
wood effect technique *20*, 52, 71, 71–2, *122*
  fantasy grain 72

List of Suppliers

Manufacturers or Suppliers whose products I use all the time:

DULUX
ICI Paints Division
Wexham Road
Slough
Middlesex

0753 31151

Paint

CROWN
Unit 1
Lyon Trading Estate
High Street
West Drayton
Middlesex

0895 449 661

Paint

WINSOR & NEWTON
[Shop]
51 Rathbone Place
London W1

01-636 4231

[Head office]
Whitefriars Avenue
Wealdstone
Harrow
Middlesex

01-427 4343

Powders, gouaches for colouring paints, stencil card paper

HAMILTON BRUSH MANUFACTURERS
Rosslyn Crescent
Wealdstone
Harrow
Middlesex

01-427 1405

Paint brushes, fitches, fans, mops etc.

H & R JOHNSON
Highgate Works
Tunstall
Stoke on Trent
Staffordshire

0782 575575

Tiles

POTTERY CRAFT LTD
Campbell Road
Stoke on Trent
Staffordshire

0782 272444

Tile glazes

BRIAR WHEELS SUPPLIERS
Arch Farm
Whitsbury Road
Fordingbridge
Hampshire

0425 52991

Kilns and kiln equipment, and pottery craft glazes

THE FULHAM POTTERY
8–10 Ingate Place
London SW8

01-720 0050

Kilns and kiln equipment

GREEN & STONE ART SUPPLIERS
259 Kings Road
London SW3

01-352 0837

Gold powders and Dutch metal leaf

Calico – from any good department store, I use:

JOHN LEWIS
Oxford Street
London SW1

01-629 7711

Varnish – I use Ronseal, from any hardware, home decorating or DIY store

Sponges – natural: from any good chemist/pharmacist or art supplier Synthetic or car sponges: garage forecourts, gas stations or hardware stores

Lining paper – any good home decorating or DIY store

USA

GLIDDEN COATINGS AND RESINS
925 Euclid Avenue
Cleveland
Ohio 44115

216 344 8156

Suppliers of Dulux paints

WINSOR & NEWTON INC
555 Winsor Drive
Secaucus
New Jersey 07094

201 864 9100

Powders, gouaches for colouring paints, stencil card paper

H & R JOHNSON INC
State Highway 35
Keyport
New Jersey 07735

201 264 0566

Tiles

CUTTER CERAMICS
47 Athletic Field Road
Waltham
Massachusetts 02154

617 893 1200

Suppliers of Pottery Craft products